Old Folks at Home

Alvin Rabushka
and
Bruce Jacobs

F P

THE FREE PRESS
A Division of Macmillan Publishing Co., Inc.
NEW YORK

Collier Macmillan Publishers
LONDON

To our parents
and the memory of our grandparents,
with the respect they deserve

The Free Press
A Division of Macmillan Publishing Co., Inc.
866 Third Avenue, New York, N.Y. 10022

Collier Macmillan Canada, Ltd.

Library of Congress Catalog Card Number: 79-7637

Printed in the United States of America

printing number

1 2 3 4 5 6 7 8 9 10

Library of Congress Cataloging in Publication Data

Rabushka, Alvin.
    Old folks at home.

    Bibliography: p.
    Includes index.
    1. Aged--United States--Economic conditions.
2. Aged--United States--Social conditions. 3. Aged
--United States. I. Jacobs, Bruce   joint
author. II. Title.
HQ1064.U5R3 1980   301.43'5'0973   79-7637
ISBN 0-02-925670-4

Contents

Preface and Acknowledgments *v*

Part One   OLD FOLKS

One   FACTS AND FALLACIES ON AGING *3*

Two   THE AGED COME OF AGE *19*

Three   THE FACTS ON OLD FOLKS AT HOME *34*

Part Two   AT HOME

Four   HOW THE ELDERLY SEE THEIR HOUSING *69*

Five   THE EXPERTS' VIEW *85*

Six   LAY VERSUS EXPERT *124*

Part Three   WHAT NEXT?

Seven   WHAT'S IN THE WAY? *135*

Eight   WHAT'S TO BE DONE? *153*

Appendixes

A. Sampling Procedure   171
B. Housing Evaluation Form   173
C. A Statistical Explanation of Housing Condition   176

Notes   181

Select List of References on Aging   197

Index   199

Preface and Acknowledgments

THERE IS A STANDARD VIEW of aging in America which holds that a great many of the elderly are helpless—in desperate need of money, meals, housing, health care, and other services. We contend that this view is erroneous, contradicted by the facts of aging. *Old Folks at Home* grew from the conviction that national debate and discussion on the choice of appropriate policies and programs for the elderly would benefit from a straightforward presentation of the condition of most older Americans. They are, for the most part, self-supporting adults, who live in dignity and independence.

Over the past five years, a large number of people contributed their assistance to this study and we want to take this opportunity to thank them. We thank Roberta J. Warren, for managing the field survey, which was carried out by the TransCentury Corporation; Sandra Hendricks, for help in preparation of the questionnaire; Patricia Greenfield and Samuel Ofsevit, for assistance in drawing the sample; Bonnie Daniels and Kathleen Yordi, who trained the field staff; Susan Mello, who supervised the coding process; Steven Marcus, who put thousands of bits of information into accessible computer tapes; and, the site managers, interviewers, and housing evaluators, who ably carried out complicated field procedures. Most of all, we want to thank the 1,575 elderly homeowners who opened their lives and homes to us for several hours.

Several of our colleagues read, in whole or in part, an

earlier draft of the manuscript and offered us the benefit of their criticisms. First among equals is Robert Hessen, whose careful reading and valuable comments greatly improved our book. Other helpful comments and suggestions were given by Martin Anderson, Rita Ricardo Campbell, Barry Chiswick, Richard F. Fenno, Jr., Roger A. Freeman, Eric A. Hanushek, Sidney Hook, Richard F. Muth, Hugh O. Nourse, and Dan Throop Smith.

Financial support for the data collection phase and initial analysis of the study came from the U.S. Department of Housing and Urban Development, and we thank HUD for the opportunity to carry out a large scale study of the nation's elderly homeowners. Subsequent analysis and final work on the manuscript was completed at the Hoover Institution with support from the Domestic Studies Program, and The University of Rochester with support from the Public Policy Analysis Program. Typing of both the preliminary and final drafts of the manuscript was ably performed by Ilse Dignam.

We gratefully acknowledge the help from all these sources, who are, of course, not responsible for any errors the book may contain.

Finally, some words about the purpose and format of the book. The issues we address should be of concern to both the general public and those with a more specialized interest in the subjects of aging, housing, and public policy in general. For purposes of readability, we have placed as much of the technical discussion as possible in the appendixes. The sources of facts, figures, and quotations that appear in the text are identified in the notes at the end of the book.

PART ONE

Old Folks

1

Facts and Fallacies on Aging

THE PROBLEMS OF AGING in America affect almost everyone. Many of us have aging parents and grandparents whom we know and love dearly. And most of us pay taxes that support one or more of a myriad of government programs for the aged. Indeed, federal expenditures on elderly Americans accounted for $112 billion in 1978, nearly one-quarter of the entire federal budget, and in that year Secretary of Health, Education and Welfare Joseph A. Califano, Jr., projected that spending on the older population would exceed $150 billion of the 1979 fiscal year budget of $500 billion. An analysis of future demographic trends indicates that spending to maintain current federal benefits for the aging could well account for more than 40 percent of all federal expenditures early in the next century.

As a topic of nationwide interest, old people receive more and more attention in the daily press, on radio and television, in the college classroom, and among government officials. *Time* devoted its June 2, 1975, cover story to "Old Age: How to Help Our Parents." Two years later, its editors produced another cover story entitled "Revolt of the Old: The Battle Over Forced Retirement." Competing to inform the American public on this subject, *Newsweek* entitled its cover story of February 28, 1977, "The Graying of America." Its staff writers questioned whether America could bear the cost of caring for a burgeoning older population. By late

3

1978, *The New Republic* and *National Journal* had made the elderly the subjects of cover stories. Throughout the 1970s, each of the major television networks has run special features and documentaries on the problems of the elderly. Congressional committees have disclosed nursing home scandals, fraudulent insurance practices targeted at elderly widows, the presence of hunger and poverty, and rampant criminal victimization of our older people.

Writers, public officials, and news commentators talk with unprecedented concern about the personal, social, and economic problems that have accompanied the aging of our people, about discrimination against the elderly, about the inhumane aspects of forced retirement, inflation destroying the purchasing power of limited incomes, crime and fear, and so on. We have, as a nation, chosen the path of touting more and more problems for the elderly and have succeeded in increasing public concern about them. Yet, despite the proliferation of crisis-writing and the fact that hundreds of billions of dollars are being spent on programs for the aging, the plain truth is that we know very little about the majority of older Americans, those who live in their own homes.

Those who write about the special problems of a particular group in society often make their case with extraordinary examples of misfortune. This creates an impression that the members of this group are different from the rest of us, indeed foreigners to our everyday lives. Some writers correctly portray the elderly as victims of poverty and unscrupulous nursing home operators, but this description fits only a small minority of them. It distorts what should be our perception of the vast majority of the aged, namely, that except for their age (and perhaps a few of their preferences), they are quite like the rest of us.

To begin with, less than 5 percent of those people aged 65 and over have to live in institutions. More than 95 percent live right in the community with us, either in an apartment or in their own home. Most live in homes that are mortgage-free. In fact, 70 per cent of all elderly householders live in their own homes, compared with only 63 percent for the under-65 population. This percentage represents more than nine million homes, or just about one-fifth of all homes owned in the U.S. This is equal to the total number of owner-occupied homes in the states of New York, California, Illinois, and Texas combined. The value of these homes exceeds $300 billion and is inflating rapidly. While a small number of institutionalized and unfortunate elderly receive the lion's share of public attention, the vast majority of older Americans are seldom discussed. And when they are discussed, it is all too often in the same breath as the small minority of utterly dependent to whom the unpleasant stereotypes most accurately apply.

In both the popular and academic press one finds a very disheartening but standard treatment of elderly homeowners, consisting of a litany of ills that afflict old people: inadequate income, bodily and mental degeneration, oversized older homes in need of substantial maintenance and repair, changing neighborhood conditions, social isolation, and forced retirement. Let's take these one at a time.

The Standard View

Income. A leading textbook writer in the field of social gerontology asserts that the single most demoralizing fact of life for most older people is that they are poor. Taking the poverty level in 1967 at $3,000 for married couples and $2,000 for single persons, he writes that 60 percent of older Americans are poor. Another author, a Pulitzer Prize winner, has written that over half of our elderly population live in deprivation, citing as evidence a United States Senate Special Committee on Aging report that about 4.8 million aged persons were living in poverty in 1969. A report produced by the Administration on Aging entitled *Facts and Figures on Older Americans* maintained that half of the more

5

than 7.2 million elderly couples had incomes below $5,000 and that half of the 5.8 million older people living alone had incomes below $2,000 in 1970. And the 1973 *Annual Housing Survey* reported that 56 percent of all families who live in their own homes and whose incomes are less than $5,000 have an aged head: This statistic means that among all homeowners, the majority of those with low incomes are aged.

Declining health. The standard view also holds that the elderly are far more likely to suffer from disease or disabling conditions than younger people. At least one in five older persons suffers from heart condition, hypertension, or loss of sight or hearing. Fully 38 percent are afflicted with arthritis or rheumatism. All told, 85 percent report at least one chronic condition. Failing health is especially precipitous for those over 75, who are more susceptible to illness. Aging is also accompanied by declining physical capacity, which impedes independent living and makes home ownership a growing burden. The National Center for Health Statistics reported in 1974 that 44 percent of all elderly people have some activity limitations (compared with 9 percent in the 17–44 age group and 23 percent in the 45–64 group). And, more than any other group, older people need medical care, and those costs are rapidly escalating.

Deteriorating housing. The single most striking fact about homes owned by the elderly is that they are old homes: The *1970 Census of Housing* revealed that 88 percent of all elderly families lived in houses built before 1960 and over half in pre–World War II units. Almost half of these families have not moved in the last thirty years and often live in big houses, burdensome to clean and maintain. Being older, this housing is also worth less than newer homes occupied by younger persons. In 1970, for example, 57 percent of homes belonging to the elderly were worth less than

$15,000; 34 percent were worth less than $10,000. These percentages are nearly double those for younger homeowners. Property values have risen dramatically in recent years, but this does little to reduce maintenance requirements, and although most older homeowners meet no monthly mortgage or rental payments, they often cannot afford to sell and move elsewhere because most suitable housing alternatives cost more. Many elderly also live in rural areas, and these homes are typically least up-to-date; in 1970, 90 percent of all homes without flush toilets could be found in rural areas.

Rising costs. Housing costs typically rise more rapidly than other costs. This rise, it is argued, most harshly affects the elderly, who must live on limited, fixed incomes. Between 1950 and 1970, the Consumer Price Index rose 61 percent, while its housing component rose by 63 percent. Since 1970, housing prices have risen even more rapidly than other prices. A 1977 Congressional Budget Office study found that total monthly housing costs have risen from $217 in 1970 to $396 in 1975, which is an increase of 82 percent; during the same period, property taxes rose 105 percent, insurance costs rose 89 percent, and maintenance and repair costs rose 118 percent.

Geographical mobility. By and large, the elderly stay put. Nearly half of all elderly homeowners have lived in the same house for three decades. To some, this implies that many elderly may be trapped in their old homes, either because they can't afford a new, smaller house in the suburbs, or because they cannot tear up a lifetime of neighborhood roots.

Social isolation. Such severe physical decline as being immobilized by arthritis or paralyzed by a stroke may also inflict the pain of social isolation. Physical incapacity limits social activity with the outside world: shopping, entertain-

7

ment, visiting friends. Blindness and loss of speech frustrate the older person's ability to communicate with his or her network of acquaintances. Social isolation may also result from nonphysical causes. The death of family members breaks close ties of lifelong duration, which may be impossible to replace. Changes in familiar friendship patterns and in the neighborhood may also induce further withdrawal. Fear of crime may limit outings to certain safe daylight periods. All the while, despite urgings from children and well-intentioned friends, most elderly are unwilling to move from the house they have known and loved for half of their lives. "Life is lived in a kind of solitary confinement destructive to mental and physical health and to humanity."

Employment. About 20 percent of older men and 8 percent of older women actively work, but typically in low-paying jobs; many work only part-time, or in agriculture or self-employed jobs. The transition from a lifetime of work to forced retirement reduces income and personal satisfaction and may bring on feelings of uselessness, resentment, and animosity.

The standard view of elderly homeowners conveys a negative image, an image that focuses largely on their needs and problems. As television brings home the agonies suffered by some elderly men and women in nursing homes, in shabby hotels, as victims of fraud and crime, the long-standing negative images of aging are reinforced. These images hold that to be old is to be helpless, useless, dependent, and unhappy—and even rigid, cantankerous, and resentful. In the view of Dr. Robert Butler, director of the National Institute on Aging, "For the most part the elderly struggle to exist in an inhospitable world." Older Americans can only look forward to "The Tragedy of Old Age in America."

Those who find this standard view compelling forcefully argue the need for new and expanded programs on aging. Butler's Pulitzer-Prize winning book contains a list of recommendations to alleviate the plight of the aging. He advocates measures such as the establishment of a universal pension system tied to the cost of living and the nation's productivity, massive housing production, an enforceable legal right to services, comprehensive medical care, a Commission on Mental Health and Illness for the Elderly, strong legislation to control quackery, and other programs.

An Alternative View

Our support for actual and proposed public programs on aging is largely conditioned by our perceptions of the needs and problems of the elderly. How tragic if that perception—the perception we have just described—is inaccurate! But, we contend, the standard view *is* largely inaccurate and *is* inappropriate as a basis on which to fashion and deliver programs for the aging, especially for the elderly homeowners who are 70 percent of our entire aged population. Let's retrace our steps through the preceding portrait of the elderly.

Income. Between 1959 and 1977, the number of officially counted "poor" elderly dropped from 8.7 to 3.2 million, or from 33 percent of the elderly population to 14 percent. When such government services and transfer payments as Medicare, Medicaid, public housing, and double exemptions are included, the number of officially "poor" families falls even further to only 6 percent of the elderly population. From the mid-1960s to 1977, median family income for the elderly has risen from 50 percent of the national average to 57 percent; for singles, the corresponding percentage in 1977 is 65. Most elderly persons can maintain the same living standard on lower incomes because Social Security payments, indexed to keep pace with inflation, are tax free. Moreover, taxes are lower, few elderly have dependent children to support, 80 per cent have no mortgage payments to meet, and for most, work-related expenses have disappeared. If 60 percent of former income is sufficient to sustain pre-retirement living standards, then most elderly have adequate incomes. Studies of housing values also show that homes built before 1970 have risen in value by 15 percent each year between 1970 and 1973, compared with a 10 percent annual appreciation for newer homes built after 1970. Thus, elderly homeowners have built up their equity assets throughout the 1970s.

Declining health. Many elderly do have some activity limitation, but severe decline sets in systematically only for those two million persons over 85, just over 8 percent of the older population. Numerous studies show that chronological aging from 60 to 85 does not necessarily diminish interests and activities. As a concrete example, older Americans register and vote with greater regularity than newly enfranchised youngsters. The plain truth is that the overwhelming majority of old people in America are well, not sick. Most men and women over 65 can continue normal living; of the 15 percent who cannot, about one-third are taken care of in institutions. On average, older people spend less than fifteen days a year in bed due to illness. Even though surveys show that three-quarters of the elderly acknowledge a chronic health problem, the same surveys also show that 80 percent of all aged say their health is excellent, good, or fair—only 20 percent claim poor health. If well-being is a state of mind, then the vast majority of elderly are sound. Improvements in income, medical care, and insurance will likely further improve this condition of well-being.

Deteriorating housing. It should surely come as no surprise that elderly people live in older homes, since most people typically purchase their homes some thirty or more years before they retire. But older housing is not at all synonymous with deteriorating housing. In fact, in recent years older homes have been appreciating more rapidly than newer homes. Martin Mayer writes, "But for the young couples now crowding the market, the bottom line is that all those people older than themselves are now so well housed because they bought years ago." Older people are less concerned with the resale value or future occupancy of their homes. The key question is whether their homes can provide safe and suitable accommodation in later life. Evidence produced from the nationwide *Annual Housing Survey* suggests that each year housing quality is improving, not declining. The same survey also shows that the elderly are almost as well housed as the population at large, with the lion's share of structural problems found in rural areas. The fact that elderly people live in older homes thus does not mean they live in unsafe or unsuitable housing.

Rising costs. Inflation affects young and old Americans alike. But the elderly are reasonably well cushioned to cope with its distorting and damaging consequences. Social Security payments, which are tax free, are indexed to keep pace with inflation. Elderly people also enjoy a growing number of special tax benefits and discounts on private and public services. Property tax relief programs in all fifty states specifically assist senior citizens with a portion, and in some cases all, of this financial burden. A survey conducted quarterly by the federal government on residential alterations, additions, repairs, and maintenance shows that older people only spend about two-thirds as much as families under 65; yet their homes show no more deterioration than those of younger families. In 1974, the worst year of inflation in forty years, only 15 percent of older Americans told a Louis Harris survey team that they had very serious money problems.

Mobility. The elderly stay in their homes largely out of free choice. Survey evidence does not support the thesis of forced home ownership, or forced overhousing. Most elderly homeowners like their homes and the living space they afford. Most have no wish to move, but they have become somewhat less satisfied with their neighborhoods and communities; in particular, they are very much concerned about crime, racial tension, and urban blight. They wish strongly for increased security, both in their homes and in the streets.

Social isolation. For many elderly, social isolation is more apparent than real. A comprehensive analysis of fifty-five books and articles on the subjects of involuntary social isolation and voluntary withdrawal of the elderly concluded that little consensus prevails on its definition, its principal causes, the severity of its consequences, and what programs might effectively counter it. Some studies even show that most older people prefer a measure of separation from their children, even if they have enjoyed a lifetime of close ties. The 1974 Harris survey found that of all older Americans with living children, 80 percent had seen them within the past week, and over half within the last day!

Employment. Although the compulsory retirement of American workers at age 65 is now illegal, the fact of the matter is that workers have been retiring at earlier ages. In 1950 almost half of all elderly men were employed. This proportion fell to one-third by 1960 and to just over one-fifth in 1975. This decline is due to the attractiveness of the increasingly higher benefit levels available in the Social Security program, and also to a drop in self-employment. In 1961, for example, about 53 percent of the initial applicants for Social Security retirement benefits were under 65. As of 1976, fully three-fourths sought the reduced benefits available to those aged 62 to 64. Older persons are not likely to reenter the labor market in great numbers unless retirement becomes economically less attractive.

Political investigations and the touting of crises create an impression of a large number of problems and unmet needs of the elderly. But this impression applies only to a small number of elderly, and an even smaller number of elderly homeowners. It is true that some of the elderly are in financial, physical, mental, or medical distress and genuinely need assistance from government and private or church-related organizations, but a few is not 90 percent. Carefully designed programs for this small community must not be equated with comprehensive programs for all the elderly. The realization that we are talking about a minority of old folks requires a very mature sense of program design and delivery to insure that those who truly need help receive it, and that money, manpower, and time are not wasted on those who neither want nor need help.

The overwhelming majority of elderly live free from crises. Normal living is the factually correct and, we contend, most sensible way to characterize the aged and avoid the distorted and somewhat condescending images so many have professed in their advocacy of comprehensive programs on behalf of the aging. And, as we show throughout this book, when the elderly are asked to speak for themselves, the image most put forth is one of normal living, not that of perpetual crisis.

Thinking About Aging

The tarnished image of aging owes much to the sensationalism of the publicity accorded the horror stories that have emerged from public exposés of nursing homes, insurance fraud, hunger, illness, and other examples of personal misfortune. It is our contention, though, that these heavily publicized stories misrepresent the general picture of aging in America. With few exceptions, old folks are just like young folks. True, they have lived longer. And they have less money to spend, though they typically need less upon retirement. Otherwise, they are responsive to the same kinds of fears, aspirations, wishes, and concerns that face the rest

13

of us. As we think about aging, it is important to look at the elderly as we look at people of all ages. If some have specific physical, mental, or financial handicaps, so too do people of all ages. Excessive restatement of the problems of aging, rather than dispassionate identification of problems of some people who happen to be over 65 years of age, distorts our perceptions of older people. One undesirable by-product of intense focus on the problems of aging is the general view that many older people cannot fend for themselves, can no longer make important decisions, and should not have to bear individual responsibility for past or present decisions. This is a distorted view that encourages and reinforces an ever-growing and sometimes bewildering array of programs that supply a broad range of social services to millions of elderly persons. The problem is that many of these services are of little value to those older persons who neither want nor receive them.

Those who are indigent, ill, in need of shelter, or incapable of independent living, whether young or old, represent legitimate targets of public and private concern. By the same token, those elderly who are well fed, well housed, well clothed, and able to maintain independent living do not warrant public concern and large government subsidies simply to reward long life.

How might we usefully characterize elderly homeowners? Basically, old folks are as different among themselves as younger people. The elderly homeowner is not easily pigeonholed into one convenient national image. Some are white, some black. Some live in cities, others in suburbs and rural areas. Although retirement havens are largely Sunbelt communities, the elderly can be found in every state in the union and, like the population at large, are most numerous in the largest states. A cross-section of older Americans reveals the same variety that makes up the diverse regions and cultural backgrounds of this large nation. Any one stereotype of an elderly American must be misleading.

We argue that it is important to inform our understand-

14

ing of aging and our assessment of the many programs for the aged with the views of the elderly themselves. We might say that the problems of aging are of two kinds: those that older people say they have and those that experts think they have.

It is worth elaborating this crucial distinction as it applies to virtually all programs on aging: housing, health, visiting nurses, counseling, homemaking services, recreation, and so forth. Let's rephrase this distinction into the language of individual personal *preferences* and what are often claimed to be *objective needs* (usually determined by specialists). How does this distinction apply to the aged?

Preferences.   Every person has preferences—a variety of tastes and values over a whole range of objects such as food, beverages, clothing, automobiles, travel, and housing. These preferences may be determined or influenced by religious beliefs, the opinions of friends and neighbors, cultural traditions, upbringing, or other factors. Moreover, preferences change; people may want the same things at different times, or different things at different times.

This concept of preference contains several important features. First, it emphasizes the importance of the individual. Membership in a group may influence a person's point of view, but whenever we talk about groups and group values, all we mean is that like-minded people belong to the same group. In and of itself, a group does not have a preference apart from those of its members.

A second feature of preferences is that they are subjective, or highly personal. Except for the mentally incompetent, people know their own desires. Preferences are personal valuations about things based on the principles, values, and tastes each of us may hold. There is no correct preference for everyone, save from each person's own point of view. To say that an individual knows his own wants is not to say that he has the "truth" for others.

How do we know what these preferences are? A good

way is to observe the choices people make. The goods and services people purchase in the private supermarket or voluntarily obtain from the government list of social programs is evidence of preference.

Most people want many things to satisfy their varied desires. However, few of us can satisfy all our wants. We are, unfortunately, victims of scarcity, of limited pocketbooks. Budgetary constraints dictate competing choices: We can have a new roof or we can have a winter vacation in Florida. We cannot have both. Some people will install a new roof and others will winter in the sun. The choice each person makes reveals his or her priorities, his or her correct choice.

Needs. A different view talks in terms of needs, not preferences. Needs are the judgments of experts that establish minimum standards of basic human consumption of nutrition, medical care, income, housing, education, and so on. Dieticians list minimum daily food requirements, doctors identify acceptable levels of medical care, housing experts publish building codes and housing codes to which buildings must conform, educators insist on compulsory schooling for all till age 16. In each area specialists try to define or estimate an *objective need* that satisfies their minimum standard of human well-being.

The judgments of lay people and experts sometimes clash, sometimes converge. One important difference between lay and expert judgments is that ordinary people face a real budget constraint in meeting their wants; expert judgments are often based on abstract criteria unencumbered by considerations of cost. Even if each person accepted the consensus of expert opinion, limited funds might preclude consumption of food, shelter, or other goods at these necessary levels.

But the matter of free choice is even more important. Experts may conclude that a home needs a new roof, but the owner may conclude that he prefers to vacation in Florida. We argue that what is objectively correct to the expert may be and indeed in this case is wrong to the traveler; what is correct for the traveler is wrong to the expert.

Granted that no standard of minimum vacation needs exists, yet the argument applies equally to clothing, food, housing, education—or any other aspect of normal living. Despite the best efforts of educators and counselors to get people in the right track in personal habits, many still do not eat right, exercise, get enough rest, or otherwise do what the experts claim is best. The essence of a free society is that people have the right to make their own choices, so long as these are not at public expense. Perhaps the gap between what people believe and do and what experts want them to believe and do partially explains the failure of so many contemporary social programs and why the experts can still point to unfilled basic needs.

A good part of this book is about old folks in their own homes. An analysis of housing quality or condition may be a good way to illustrate concretely the distinction between *preferences*, lay wants, and *needs*, the judgments of experts.

Start with each elderly individual, who determines for himself (or herself) what kind of housing he wants to inhabit and the condition in which he wants to maintain it. Depending on his budget, the amount of time, effort, and money he puts into home upkeep is the choice of each individual homeowner. That is to say, on the basis of his own personal housing standards, each homeowner must decide how much time and money to spend on housing. Of course, different people use different standards to reach different conclusions. But from the standpoint of the individual homeowner there is no such thing as an objectively correct need for the amount and quality of housing he consumes, except what he chooses for himself.

Take the specific case of home repairs and maintenance. Not only must each person identify parts of his home in need of repairs, he must also decide how much money he wants to spend, an amount that differs among individuals. Some homeowners may overlook a problem they think needs fixing because they are unwilling to invest the necessary time or money. This may be so for several reasons. A deteriorating neighborhod may defeat the benefits of diligent home maintenance, or homes may be too large with unneeded rooms, or an elderly person may decide it is not good economics to replace galvanized piping with copper because he cannot see twenty years into the future. More important, and perhaps most difficult to grasp, some individuals may accept the present condition of their house as perfectly adequate even when others might find it unsatisfactory.

The alternative to homeowner preferences is the housing expert's estimate of objective need for repairs or maintenance. For several decades the census bureau has tried to develop reliable indicators of housing quality to estimate the nation's stock of substandard housing, and since 1973 the government has conducted an annual housing survey in search of an accurate measure and estimate of housing and neighborhood quality (see Chapter 5).

It is thus possible to talk about housing, housing condition and quality, or housing standards from two standpoints—the subjective preferences of the individual homeowner and the objectively determined needs disclosed by the housing expert. No difficulty in defining a housing problem exists where the two judgments converge. When they diverge we face a serious choice over which view should prevail. Potentially the stakes involve millions of people and homes and billions of taxpayers' dollars.

2

The Aged Come of Age

Enactment of Social Security in 1935 was essentially the beginning of the national government's involvement in the problems of the dependent aged and the unemployed. In a fundamental departure from the view that old age and employment security are needs properly dealt with through individual effort and private charity (with emergency supplemental help from local government), the Roosevelt New Deal undertook to erect a structure of financial protection, the revenues for which would be generated from a tax on worker payrolls and employers.

Henry J. Pratt in *The Gray Lobby*

BY AND LARGE, Americans take Social Security for granted. Although enacted only forty-five years ago, it is the most sacrosanct of all government programs, especially among elderly voters. It is the subject of burgeoning public interest, as well as recent congressional legislation in light of the system's diminishing financial reserves and threats to its solvency in the remaining decades of this century. Few politicians dare question the worth of the program in public, and those who do are ill-advised. The most recent public figure to propose serious changes in the system was Ronald Reagan during the 1976 Republican presidential primary in Florida. Reagan lost the Florida primary election and ultimately his party's nomination to Gerald Ford. Twelve years earlier,

Senator Barry Goldwater of Arizona, the Republican presidential nominee in 1964, encountered a similar fate when he questioned compulsory Social Security. A study of the 1964 election disclosed that a substantial majority of voters over 60 went for Johnson; in all, some two million traditional Republicans switched their votes. These older adults contributed to Johnson's landslide victory.

Social Security payments are an extremely important segment of the total federal budget. Social Security outlays grow by leaps and bounds—from $67 billion in 1975, to $83 billion in 1977, to $100 billion in the 1979 fiscal year budget. These outlays make up 21 percent of all federal expenditure; Social Security taxes and contributions, in turn, constitute fully 28 percent of all government receipts. Even taking inflation into account, benefit levels have risen so that the retirement benefits of American workers have more than doubled since 1945. Talk of budget-busting due to spending on the elderly makes aging a subject of growing national interest.

The Elderly Population Explosion

"Every day, approximately 5,000 Americans celebrate their sixty-fifth birthday. Every day, approximately 3,600 persons aged 65 or older die. The *net* increase is about 1,400 a day, or a half million a year." Experts estimate the 1977 65-plus population at 23.5 million, or roughly 11 percent of the total population.

The aging of America is unique to the twentieth century. When the colonies declared independence in 1776, those over 65 numbered only fifty thousand, or 2 percent of fledgling America; by 1900 their number had risen to three million, comprising 4 percent. Since 1900 the elderly population has grown sevenfold (compared with a threefold increase for the overall population), and the percentage growth in the elderly population continues to outpace that of the under-65. Projections through the year 2040 place the total number of elderly at fifty million and, depending on the birth rate, at somewhere between 16 and 20 percent of all Americans. It may be relevant for social policy, and for the financial viability of the Social Security system, that younger people under 18 are a declining proportion of the total population, while those over 65 enjoy uninterrupted increase.

Life expectancy. Life expectancy at birth for American males is 69 years, for females 77 years. At the turn of the century the corresponding figures were 48 and 51 years. Today's child can expect to live nearly a quarter of a century longer than his great-grandparents. Moreover, life expectancy has increased at every age level. Due mainly to medical advances, especially in the treatment of heart disease, those who reach 60, 70, or 80 can expect more remaining years of life than their nineteenth century counterparts. Improved diet and exercise, along with better medical care, foreshadow still further increases in life expectancy in the future.

The transition from a life that was nasty, brutish, and, especially, short to comfort and old-age is relatively recent. Life expectancy recorded few gains all the way from the era of prehistoric man up through the nineteenth century. Prehistoric man rarely lived past 40; the normal life span of early tribes and of Neanderthal man was between the late teens and late twenties. Life expectancy remained fairly constant between the Neanderthal man of 150,000 years ago and early sedentary societies of 10,000 years ago; fewer than 10 percent of these newer sedentary men lived past 40 and virtually no one made it to 50.

By the fifth century B.C., average life span had increased to about 30 years, but if a person could survive the hazards of childhood, he could look forward to a much longer life than the average for his time. A classical Greek of 680 B.C. who survived to age 15 would live another 41 years. An imperial Roman of A.D. 120 enjoyed almost equal longevity. From the pre-Greek civilization of 3,500 B.C. through the

Romantic era of A.D. 1750, expectation of life ranged from a low of an additional 31 to a high of 41 years, providing you survived the first 15. In each era some individuals lived 70, 80, or 90 years, but high infant mortality meant these survivors and generally those who reached 40 years of age were few in number.

Life expectancy in colonial America fell far short of today's 70-plus years. In eighteenth century Massachusetts and New Hampshire, for instance, life expectancy at birth was only 28 years. When the first federal census was taken in 1790, less than 20 percent of the American population had survived from birth to age 70 (compared with a figure of 80 percent today).

Starting in the eighteenth century, improvements in food, housing, medical care, and sanitation steadily lowered mortality rates. A rising standard of living, brought about in the course of the industrial revolution, enabled more and more people to survive to old age. The combination of greater longevity and falling birth rates, which began in the nineteenth century, brought about the eventual aging of the entire population: The median age of Americans in 1790 was barely 16; it is now 30.

The Growth of Aging as a Subject for Study

Gerontology, the study of the aging process, has come into prominence as an important field of theoretical and applied study since the end of the Second World War. Philosophers and scholars throughout the ages have puzzled over the secrets of prolonging life; adventurers have pursued fountains of youth. Serious study of longevity was first undertaken by Roger Bacon in the thirteenth century. Other distinguished scientists extended this initial work: the astronomer Halley, the Belgian mathematician Quetelet, and a Russian physician named Fisher. These men tried to describe the physical, mental, and environmental factors associated with long life.

Isolated investigations of the aging process were transformed into gerontology as a separate field by late nineteenth and early twentieth century scholars. But intellectual inquiry still lagged behind the old-age pension and social movements of Europe and, later, America. Old-age pensions finally came to America when President Roosevelt signed the Social Security Act on August 14, 1935, but the Gerontological Society was not yet founded for another decade, till the close of World War II, at which time the *Journal of Gerontology* also began publication.

In the last quarter of the twentieth century, social gerontology has become one of the fastest-growing fields of social studies. Before 1940, only a handful of books and articles were published on the subject of aging. Forty years later, this handful has turned into an annual flood of books and articles, several thousand in number. A bibliography of titles published between 1954 and 1974 contained over fifty thousand entries on aging, and one directory listed 1,275 separate programs on aging in American educational institutions in 1975.

Now there are thousands of public and private organizations that focus wholly or partly on aging. The biggest is the nine-million-member American Association of Retired Persons, founded over twenty years ago, followed by other mainstays of the "gray lobby": the National Retired Teachers Association, the National Council on Senior Citizens, and the appropriately symbolic Gray Panthers. Other academic, advocacy, professional, or membership organizations include the American Aging Association, the American Geriatrics Society, the National Association of Retired Federal Employees, the National Caucus on the Black Aged, the National Center on Black Aged, and the National Council on the Aging; and handbooks list dozens of additional similar organizations.

Government Interest in Aging

Burgeoning intellectual interest in aging has been outpaced by an even more dramatic expansion in government programs and public spending. The first public commission on aging was founded in 1909 by the state of Massachusetts. By 1975, some sixty-six years later, a Select Committee on Aging in the House of Representatives counted 134 federal programs on aging that touched the responsibilities of forty-nine congressional committees and subcommittees. Its counterpart body in the United States Senate estimated in 1975 that some 330,000 people directly earned their living providing basic services to the elderly, compared to a handful before World War II.

But for three centuries following the settlement of Jamestown in 1607, America neither legislated nor spent public monies on its aged population. In keeping with the conservative ethos of American politics, government at all levels rarely intruded into the personal affairs of private citizens. This ethic applied to the young and old alike. The colonial and early independence practice of non-intervention gave way to government assistance only after President Roosevelt's New Deal.

What smoothed the way for growing public action for aging? Growth in longevity and in sheer numbers of the elderly played an important role in this transition. Gray power is a direct consequence of a politically and numerically significant number of elderly people, who make up an ever-greater share of the population with each passing decade.

A second factor was the rise of elderly unemployment. Self-support among old people has always been the rule throughout history. Earlier civilizations distinguished only the frail and infirm as a social group deserving public concern. The able-bodied elderly maintained their working role and were not deemed as needing or deserving retirement in the modern sense. Indeed, those who worked in various social, economic, or political positions did not retire; they usually died in office.

David Fischer has described the living conditions of old people at the time of colonial New England. In normal circumstances, ministers worked until they died. Retirement as an age-determined formal requirement or general expectation did not exist. Old men were expected to remain self-supporting in gainful employment as long as they could.

Ministers were like members of any other occupation. Schoolmasters, businessmen, and political leaders all died on the job, sometimes quite literally at their desks. Five of the six governors of Plymouth Colony served into old age, and four died in office.

Compulsory retirement was unknown in America until 1790, after which some state legislatures specified age limits for public servants, initially to discharge senile judges. Although retirement gradually spread to other fields throughout the nineteenth century, the majority of men remained actively at work. Three-fourths of all men over 65 earned their keep in 1870. The business practice of mandatory retirement did not appear until the middle decades of the twentieth century. Retirement as an idea and a way of life finally arose in the twentieth century because the average age of death extended beyond the typical worker's productive economic life. This growth in retirees was helped along by labor union practices, which sought to establish a stable retirement system for those over 65 to protect jobs for middle-aged workers. A growing life span coupled with the practice of fixed retirement at 65 generated rapid increases in elderly unemployment. In 1900, close to two-thirds of older men were still working; by 1950, this fraction fell to one-half; today it is only one-fifth.

Longevity alone does not account for the explosive growth in retirees. Rapid economic growth since World War

25

II created the prosperity that enabled government to legislate an increasingly attractive system of retirement benefits. Rising benefit levels have induced more and more early retirements, but we should not forget that it was the Depression that spawned the old-age political movements and a growing spate of national legislation stemming from Social Security. The Depression produced widespread national unemployment, but it hit the aged especially hard. Old-age dependency, estimated at 23 percent of the aged in 1910, had reached 50 percent by the height of the Depression. Social Security was initially conceived to guarantee income in old age that was no longer available in a Depression world of diminishing employment opportunities, even though its attractive benefits may now be the greatest cause of elderly unemployment.

A consequence of pervasive government involvement in the lives of older people is a shift in living arrangements. In colonial America, very few old people lived alone. Men and women lived with their unmarried children until they died in their fifties, which typically coincided with the completion of child rearing. Three-generation households were rare. Where they existed, it was usually the young who were dependent not the old.

Now, more and more old people live alone. In 1940, 35 percent of all elderly persons (our grandparents) lived either with their own children or a relative; by 1970, only 13 percent did so. Today's elderly have more money, enjoy better health, and are better educated than their predecessors. The robust postwar economy enabled most of them to build or buy a home, and Social Security and pension checks allow the great majority to maintain themselves and their homes on their own, without help from their children.

Growth in solitary residence of aged couples and individuals went hand in hand with greater geographic mobility for all persons. In early America, relatives lived together in neighborhoods, creating a sense of extended family. Distances between the aged and their children have grown, although social ties remain strong. For some well-to-do aged this process has culminated in age-segregated retirement villages, in which children are no more than occasional guests.

History of old-age assistance. In ancient times, public and private organizations provided assistance for those elderly infirm who lacked family support, although on a very limited scale. In the third and fourth centuries, for example, the Christian church in the Middle East established institutions for the needy aged called "gerontochia." Gradually these institutions spread throughout western Europe. In medieval times, the sick and elderly were cared for by their feudal lord or in the monasteries. In Britain, almshouses were established as early as A.D. 1136 and provided modest relief for several centuries.

Religious disputes in the sixteenth century throttled the growth in monastic care of the elderly; in its place, local parishes opened "poorhouses" in the seventeenth century, which were supported by local ratepayers (taxpayers). Throughout the seventeenth, eighteenth, and nineteenth centuries the aged in Britain were looked after by either their families or their employers, supported by private charity, or—under the Poor Law—received parish relief or entered the poorhouse.

Large-scale government action on behalf of aged persons came to western Europe decades before it arrived on American shores. France began to provide some old-age support as early as 1850. The first major comprehensive program for all aged persons appeared with the enactment of the German health, accident, and old-age/invalidism programs of the 1880s. In the next twenty-five years, pension schemes were set up in Denmark (1891), Belgium (1894), Austria

(1906), Britain (1908), and Sweden (1913). America joined the ranks in 1935, nearly half a century after Bismarck's path-breaking legislation.

Passage of Social Security opened the doors to a fast-expanding agenda of federal government activities in aging, which were nurtured by growing numbers of elderly voters. In 1950 the first national conference on aging was held; its chief recommendation was that both voluntary and government agencies accept greater responsibility for the problems and welfare of older people.

In 1956 the Senate Labor Committee created a Special Staff on Aging. About the same time, President Eisenhower formed the Federal Council on Aging, which was comprised of representatives of other federal departments that maintained programs on aging. By the mid-1950s, most states had established state units on aging and were exploring the need for local-level units. This burst of political activity culminated in the first federally financed White House Conference on Aging in 1961, which called for the establishment of a federal agency in the field of aging.

Various sourcebooks on aging, handbooks for older Americans, directories of available services, and the appendices in virtually every popular book on aging list innumerable programs and addresses where individuals and groups of elderly persons may go to get information and assistance for their various concerns. A centerpiece in this information and assistance network is a national Administration on Aging, created on passage of the Older Americans Act of 1965 and its related amendments. It sponsors a bevy of grants for state and community programs on aging, various training and research projects, and multipurpose senior centers; it feeds millions of meals through the national nutrition program for the elderly; and it supports various educational and employment opportunities. Its grants to the states and localities have created hundreds of area agencies on aging to encourage and coordinate delivery of services to the elderly by local agencies and organizations. The Administration on Aging began life in 1965 with an initial appropriation of $10 million. In the 1978 budget year, funding for the Older Americans Act totaled $509 million, a more than fiftyfold increase in just thirteen years.

Congress recently established a National Institute on Aging, the newest of the eleven National Institutes of Health. Its first director was appointed on May 1, 1976, and he has been extraordinarily successful in his budget requests. The agency received nearly $38 million from Congress for the 1978 budget year. President Carter requested the same level of funding for 1979, but Congress overrode his request and authorized $54.5 million, a sum that the President approved as he signed the 1979 Labor-HEW Appropriations Act.

Congress has been busy in other areas as well. The Supplemental Security Income (SSI) program, established in 1972, provides cash grants to about 9 percent of all older Americans whose incomes fall below the federal government's lowest definition of poverty. The Medicare and Medicaid programs were both enacted in 1965 and already pay nearly $30 billion in annual health care expenses of the elderly. Public housing projects have housed an increasing number of elderly persons in recent years: Over 40 percent of all residents in public housing are aged. Federal funds also support "Foster Grandparents," "Retired Senior Volunteer Programs," veterans programs, and $3 million is now spent to enforce the Age Discrimination in Employment Act. The 1978 Comprehensive Employment and Training Act (CETA) amendments include provisions for older workers; similarly the 1978 education amendments authorize $5 million for community education to meet the needs of middle-aged and older Americans.

Social Security payments represent the bulk of all federal outlays in aging, which increased from $25 billion in 1967, to $46 billion in 1972, to over $100 billion in 1978. If we exclude Social Security and other mandatory programs and look only at federal outlays in "discretionary" programs, we see a near tripling of expenditure between 1967 and 1972 and continuing growth through the remainder of the decade.

Local government units are active in the field of aging, sometimes with the help of federal and state revenues. For example, counties administer more than a thousand home health and homemaker/home health aide offices throughout the country. Complementing this array of public agencies are thousands of voluntary associations: senior-owned cooperatives, "rent-a-granny," meals on wheels, repairs on wheels, church organizations, and so on.

In the last fifteen years, Congress has more than overcome its historical neglect of aging. Along with its massive appropriations each year for Social Security retirement benefits, Congress votes billions of dollars for dozens of programs that serve the aging. The comprehensive scope of government activities is readily apparent in the following list of programs and their annual budgets for fiscal 1979:

- Social Security ($102 billion)
- Older Americans Act ($546 million)
  - National Information and Resource Clearing House
  - Federal Council on the Aging
  - Title III State and Community Programs on Aging
  - Title IV Research, Training, and Gerontology Centers
  - Title V Senior Centers
  - Title VII Nutrition
- Medicare ($29 billion)
- Medicaid ($8 billion)
- Senior Community Service Employment ($190 million)
- Supplemental Security Income ($5 billion)
- Housing ($800 million)
- ACTION's Older American Programs ($58 million)
  - Retired Senior Volunteer Program
  - Foster Grandparents
  - Senior Companions

- National Institute on Aging ($55 million)
- Senior Opportunities and Services ($10 million)
- Title XX Social Services ($2 billion)
- Food Stamps ($6 billion)
- Urban Mass Transportation Assistance ($28 million)
- Service Corps of Retired Executives ($2 million)

The aged have surely come of age.

For most elderly persons, Social Security payments are the primary source of income. These payments, while modest, sustain independent living in later life. Social Security does not finance an affluent retirement, but primary responsibility for support in old age no longer rests on employment, private savings, or charity. These retirement checks are augmented by a full spectrum of federal, state, and local programs for the aging that, together, go a long way to insure an acceptable standard of living. And most of these government payments and programs rise each year to keep pace with inflation.

Government, Housing, and the Aged

This is a book about old folks in their own homes. "What does housing mean to the elderly? Aside from his spouse, housing is probably the single most important element in the life of an older person."

Government intervention in housing parallels that in aging—it was negligible until modern times. Housing codes, building codes, and zoning regulations are all modern inventions. The first systematic use of zoning was the New York zoning code of 1916, which was adopted as a model code by the Department of Commerce in the 1920s and later became a model for other cities. Building codes specify the structural and mechanical integrity of new construction, including its fire resistance; model codes have been adopted in about

31

1,600 communities. Finally, housing codes set minimum standards of health and safety relating to the quality of basic facilities, level of maintenance, and occupancy of a housing unit. Until passage of the Housing Act of 1954, no more than a hundred cities had housing codes; requirements of the act encouraged their adoption, so that about five thousand local governments had housing codes by 1968.

Today, federal programs in housing number in the hundreds and their costs run in the billions. But unlike the Social Security and Older Americans Acts that concentrate monies directly on the elderly, federal housing programs only partly address the elderly. Of those programs that serve the elderly, the greatest share of public monies is spent on the 25 percent of elderly who rent rather than own. Institutional living arrangements for the elderly also receive a good deal of attention, even though they house fewer than one in twenty of all older Americans. Federal subsidy of medical costs for the elderly has been accompanied by rapid growth of day-care centers, nursing homes, and other congregate living facilities.

Elderly homeowners are eligible for only a handful of housing programs, which include rehabilitation grant and loan programs for homeowners who live in code enforcement or urban renewal areas, and small-scale assistance for local "chore service" and "Handy Andy" programs that undertake modest repairs that the elderly cannot do themselves. Rural elderly are eligible for the home repair loan program of the Farmers Home Administration, though this latter program is not widely used. All told, these programs spend no more than a few million dollars on elderly homeowners out of a total budget for federal housing programs that runs to $12 billion. It is obvious that today's better living conditions among older persons, especially homeowners, is not due to the existence of housing programs for the elderly; rather, the increased level of lifetime and retirement income is a chief cause.

Getting the Image Right

Among the elderly, many depend on the income, medical, and other benefits that Social Security, Supplemental Security Income, Medicare, Medicaid, and other public programs provide. Television, newspaper, and congressional concern with those in nursing homes, overcrowded hotels, or rural shacks engenders an image that the plight of the great majority of old people is steadily growing worse. What may be true for a minority of older citizens is most certainly not true for the vast majority. In 1980, more elderly live in their own homes, enjoy better health, and depend less on friends and family than ever before. Elderly homeowners, in particular, enjoy a standard of living and personal independence unknown to prior generations. Yet a drumbeating emphasis on bad news about America's aging may create the image of a second-class citizen at the very time that most elderly are able to deal successfully with most aspects of their lives.

All of this growing interest in, writing about, and spending on the elderly shows no signs of abatement. Because aging is the growth industry of the late twentieth century, it is especially important that public and private discussions of the aged rest upon an accurate and dispassionate view, rather than an ardent but misdirected advocacy.

3

The Facts on Old Folks at Home

IN DECEMBER 1974 the United States government commissioned a nationwide study of elderly homeowners. Of key interest was why some elderly neglect repair and maintenance of their homes, how many live in homes that have significantly deteriorated, and, what might be done to help elderly homeowners on limited incomes properly keep up their homes. The presumption was that many old folks cannot properly maintain their homes and that perhaps government ought to intensify its activities in this area.

A major focus on elderly homeowners has been long overdue. Most earlier studies and programs have concentrated on the institutionalized, on elderly who live in public housing or other special communities. One cannot draw from these studies an accurate picture of older Americans who on their own take care of themselves and their homes. These remarks are not meant to downplay the importance of eliminating harmful conditions in the nation's nursing homes, and assuring the correct design and construction of housing for handicapped or disabled elderly. Still, it is equally important that we avoid the myopic and potentially harmful view that most elderly cannot look after themselves.

At the same time that the government commissioned a survey of elderly homeowners, the National Council on the Aging asked Louis Harris and Associates to undertake the most extensive survey ever conducted on the public's attitude toward aging and its perception of what it is like to be old in this country—and to document older Americans' views and attitudes about themselves. Louis Harris and Associates conducted their survey in the early summer of 1974 and published *The Myth and Reality of Aging in America* in April 1975.

What it's like to be an elderly homeowner is the subject of this book. The survey of elderly homeowners that we conducted on behalf of the Department of Housing and Urban Development in 1975 affords a unique opportunity to probe in depth the life styles and living conditions of older America, on the one hand, and a detailed exploration of their homes, neighborhoods, and communities, on the other. Coupled with the Harris survey and findings reported in the government's annual housing surveys, we can draw a portrait of mainstream older America that both enriches our understanding and structures public debates about aging during the 1980s.

Demographics of Aging

The demographics of aging are readily available in a number of official government and private scholarly sources. These treatments, however, are of necessity shallow and do not permit an in-depth probe over a whole range of topics on aging that can only be gleaned from face-to-face interviews. Still, in-depth studies are valuable only to the extent that they accurately reflect the characteristics of the elderly population at large. It is helpful, then, to see the broader demographics of aging before proceeding on to a more intensive investigation.

Sex composition. A large majority of aged are women, which is a relatively new development. Forty years ago the number of elderly males and females was equal. Now there are 68 men to every 100 women past 65; past 75, the ratio falls to 56 men for each 100 women. Actuaries project these ratios to fall steadily into the next century. Why the sudden

35

change? Women have benefited more than men from a declining death rate, especially from childbirth. Nor do men and women uniformly succumb to the same diseases: Men die far more frequently than women from heart diseases, cancer, influenza/pneumonia, accidents, respiratory diseases, and cirrhosis of the liver. These are among the top ten causes of death among the aged. Moreover, more aged men than women suffer some activity limitation, and aged men are considerably more prone to suicide.

In 1975, therefore, the excess of elderly women over men totaled 4.1 million, compared with less than three-quarters of a million excess women in 1950. By the year 2000 the number will rise to 6.5 million. America is fast becoming a nation of widows and retired elderly women.

Marital status. As expected, many more elderly women than men live alone. In 1975 about four-fifths of all aged men were married; not even 1 percent was single; and only 16 percent were widowed or divorced. The picture was dramatically different for women: 36 percent married, 57 percent widowed or divorced, and 7 percent single. Thus, in 1975, nearly two out of every five elderly women lived alone. On average, a married woman could expect to outlive her husband by nearly eight years. Moreover, many more widowers than widows remarry.

Race. The twentieth century has witnessed a dramatic increase in the number of aged blacks. Between 1900 and 1967 the expectation of life at birth increased by nearly 29 years for black males and 35 for black females to 61 and 68 years, respectively. Still, only 7 percent of the black population (in 1975) had passed their sixty-fifth birthday compared with 11 percent among whites; for Hispanics, the figure is less than 4 percent. These disparities follow from higher fertility rates among blacks and Hispanics: Proportionally more young blacks and Hispanics are born than whites. Longevity figures are almost identical: A white male or female at age 60 can expect to live an additional 17 or 22 years; blacks expect an additional 16 or 21 years. The difference is only one year.

Geography. Old folks are most numerous in the largest states: more than two million each in New York and California, more than one million each in Pennsylvania, Florida, Illinois, Texas, and Ohio. Overall, the annual migration rate of old folks across state lines is just over 1 percent—less than half that of the general population. When they move, it is to the Sunbelt, where retirement communities flourish. Arizona, Nevada, Hawaii, and especially Florida have experienced tremendous growth in their aged populations. Florida's elderly population grew 78 percent from 1960 to 1970, by 30 percent from 1970 to 1975. (This growth will increasingly influence state politics and presidential primary elections in Florida.) But except for Florida, where the elderly now exceed 16 percent of the state's population, and Alaska (with less than 3 percent), the proportions of aged in most states hover at the national average of 10 to 11 percent.

Size of place and urban-rural residence. Within each state, where do aged persons choose to live or find themselves compelled to stay? The single largest bloc (34 percent) live in central cities. They are followed, in turn, by inhabitants of rural America (23 percent), the urban fringe (21 percent), those towns of 10,000 to 50,000 (9 percent), small towns of 2,500 to 10,000 (9 percent), and the remainder spread throughout our rural communities (4 percent). For blacks and Hispanics, the pattern differs: More than 50 percent live in central cities. On balance, a majority of elderly are scattered about the rural hinterlands or are concentrated in large urban centers, often in the deteriorating neighborhoods.

An In-Depth Investigation

We have painted, in very broad brush strokes, a demographic portrait of aging in America. But we have not yet tapped the emotions, attitudes, desires, and fears of this population. However helpful in enriching our knowledge of aging, basic demographic information does not substitute for the details of the lives of older Americans that can be acquired only by talking with them. For this we must turn to the technique of survey research.

How does one go about conducting a survey to characterize the nation's elderly homeowners? It is clearly impossible to interview more than a fraction of them. In fact, Louis Harris interviewers completed only 4,254 in-person household interviews in their massive survey, of which one-third were with persons under 65 years of age and two-thirds 65 or over. Scientific sampling techniques allow Gallup to conduct nationwide popularity polls with only 1,300 respondents and obtain results that accurately fit the entire country.

The economics of survey research reveal that it is far more expensive to sample, for example, ten people in each of one hundred communities than it is to sample one hundred people in each of ten communities. For this reason, the vast majority of in-person survey efforts limit their interviewing to a small number of survey sites. This study is no exception.

Where did we look to find a representative sample of elderly homeowners? Older Americans live in a wide variety of communities that differ in population size, region, climate, racial, or ethnic characteristics. Since interviewing and travel are costly and our budget was limited, we had to narrow our choice of communities to seven; in each of these different places we wanted to talk with 225 elderly homeowners, for a grand total of 1,575. We therefore tried to choose seven locations to reflect differences in community size, region, climate, race, culture, and the possible presence of government assistance programs.

Criteria for Site Selection

The way we chose the seven sites illustrates the research strategy we adopted. Our purpose was to select sites typical of where elderly homeowners live. Five of the seven sites were chosen from what the census bureau calls Standard Metropolitan Statistical Areas (SMSA), which are geographically demarcated areas, each with a central city of over 50,000 population. To reflect differences in community size, all 243 such areas were divided into five even strata on the basis of diminishing numbers of elderly homeowners, and one was selected from each of the five size categories. So emerged the Philadelphia SMSA among the very large cities (with 273,000 elderly home-owning families), followed by San Francisco (155,000), Dayton (42,000), Tulsa (31,000), and Pittsfield, Massachusetts (4,500). The two remaining places included one small non-SMSA urban area in Minnesota (New Ulm) with approximately 1,300 elderly homeowners, and one rural county in South Carolina (Orangeburg County) with about 3,000.

These seven sites were selected to ensure regional representation in rough proportion to where elderly homeowners live: two each from the Northeast, North Central, and South regions, and one from the West. As well, they represent modal types within regions (e.g., a rural area in the South, which has the highest proportion of rural dwelling units) and different areas within regions (e.g., a large Middle Atlantic city and a small New England urban area in the Northeast).

While not losing sight of the rich differences between communities and among old folks even in the same town or county, the task of any sample survey is to make sense of the whole. It is difficult to generalize and at the same time not oversimplify or misrepresent—to identify, simultaneously, both the unique and common aspects in the lives and homes of older Americans. The sites chosen reflect unique features in each place while at the same time disclosing a general picture of aging in America that permits national debate and discussion.

Finding the Subjects

In an ideal world we would have a list of all elderly homeowners in each site from which we could randomly select 225. In the world as we find it there are no such comprehensive lists. Indeed, how we found 225 people in each community tells a good deal about the rich variety in the lives and housing of older Americans, of differences in community norms, standards, and structures. (The details of our sampling methodology are outlined in Appendix A.)

In principle, it should be relatively easy to draw a representative sample of elderly homeowners in those communities classified as Standard Metropolitan Statistical Areas. The 1970 Census of Housing does contain information on the number of elderly residents on a block-by-block basis. In practice, however, it was not so easy. Philadelphia, the "City of Brotherly Love," was the most difficult site to sample. Philadelphians were often suspicious of strangers who knocked on their doors. We found out that many elderly homeowners were reluctant to be interviewed for our survey because fear of crime has left them wary of opening their doors. Although the full set of 225 interviews was completed, meeting the standards for scientific sampling, it tells a lot about this city that we started interviewing there first but finished there last.

A different problem cropped up in the Dayton SMSA. In order to include remote areas in the Dayton sample, U.S. Geological Survey maps that show each dwelling were acquired to supplement mapped census tracts. Prior to beginning the survey, our interviewers identified themselves at local police stations to explain what they were doing in these remote parts of the greater Dayton area. Efforts to secure police cooperation did not meet initial success: Complaints from several of the homeowners induced the police to arrest and lock up several of the interviewers. A flurry of frantic phone calls between the Washington research firm conducting the interviews, project officers in the Department of Housing and Urban Development, and a police captain in an outlying town soon cleared up the misunderstandings. Otherwise, the interviewing proceeded smoothly without event.

San Francisco typifies a different metropolitan area. Census tracts in each site were chosen to include a proportional mix of wealthy, middle-income, and lower-income elderly homeowners. In the San Francisco Bay Area, by chance, Hillsborough was picked as an upper-income tract. Bay Area residents know that Hillsborough is the premier dormitory suburb of San Francisco and home of the late Bing Crosby, William Randolph Hearst, and other prominent personalities. We do not know if these homeowners encounter any difficulties maintaining their homes, simply because neither the maids nor the butlers would allow any interviewer past the front door to interview the master of the house. Hillsborough was therefore replaced with a substitute high-income tract from the Berkeley area. Careful use of substitution procedures insured that the overall Bay Area sample remained representative.

Tulsa presented a series of contrasts as we sampled its elderly homeowners. In recent times the core city has expanded greatly and attractive new suburbs have sprouted around the city. Yet our sampling procedures also took us into more remote areas within the SMSA that contained homes quite modest in size and in ostensible need of attention. Fortunately, our local interview staff had relatively little trouble completing their work in all of these areas.

The Pittsfield SMSA is located in the beautiful hills of western Massachusetts. Here, too, we interviewed homeowners in both the central city and in outlying areas, some quite sparsely populated. In both instances we had to contend with a long tradition of independence and reticence among small-town New Englanders. Fortunately, our local staff shared these values and successfully convinced our respondents that participation in the study was not a threatening intrusion in their daily lives.

Full coverage of the entire spectrum of elderly homeowners—their lives and homes—requires travel and interviews away from the cities of America. It is not easy to draw a scientifically accurate sample of these old folks. Census tract data are not available for areas that do not include a central city of at least fifty thousand persons. Still, to represent homeowners outside standard urban areas, one site was designated for a small town and one for a purely rural area. In New Ulm, Minnesota (with a population of about thirteen thousand) we obtained from the city engineer a map of all properties within the city, which consisted of 498 blocks. Seventy-five blocks were chosen with probability proportional to the number of properties and then interviewers contacted the occupants of three elderly-owned homes on each block. New Ulm is a small town of homogeneous, largely German-descent people. The town and its people reflect this European tradition. Street layout is orderly, lot sizes are standard, buildings are generally well kept, and a statue adorns the town center to honor a German folk hero. New Ulm's elderly Americans personify small-town traits of self-reliance and community cohesion, and locally recruited interviewers had little trouble completing their work.

Orangeburg County in South Carolina was chosen to illustrate the experience of homeowners in a purely rural setting. How does one find a representative sample in a sprawling rural area? Fortunately, the South Carolina State Highway Department had prepared a general highway map of Orangeburg County, which listed every house in the county. Orangeburg County encompasses about three thousand square miles with widely spaced homes, often accessible only on dirt roads. Since there are no "blocks" outside of Orangeburg City (which was excluded from the strictly rural sample), ninety-one "tract" areas were superimposed on the map using major roads as boundaries and trying to equalize the number of homes in each "tract." From that point, sampling was routine.

Orangeburg County is as rural as one can imagine, with a population that is roughly 60 percent white and 40 percent black. Upper- and middle-income families are relatively rare, and homes do not match up to urban standards; it is almost a separate world of old homes and older people with little resemblance to urban middle-class America.

This winded sprint through seven varied sites highlights the rich diversity of American living and, as we shall see, aging. It has produced a unique but important body of information in the form of 1,575 completed interviews each involving about two hours of comprehensive yet pleasant conversation with a cross-section of elderly America. As we explain below, each of the homes we sampled was also inspected by a professional housing expert.

We talked with homeowners aged 60 years and over, rather than just those over 65. In some ways age 65 is an arbitrary dividing line against which to set off the elderly. Swedes retire at 67 and British colonial civil servants—what few remain—at 55 to 60. It is increasingly possible for municipal policemen, firemen, or sanitation men to retire at 55. And military personnel can retire with twenty years service at age 38, though full retirement at that age is rare. For many, early retirement is a reality, as more and more people opt for the reduced Social Security benefits available at age 62. Statistically, nearly one-fifth of all elderly homeowners aged 60 and over are in the 60 to 64 age bracket; they will comprise a large segment of the home-owning public as they age past 65. Their well-being today may portray tomorrow's 70- and 80-year-olds.

The Realities of Aging

Our parents are in their late fifties to late seventies; we are in our mid- to late-thirties. In the past few years, our parents have not only kept up their own homes, but helped us improve our homes as well. Among their major activities we can include interior and exterior painting, plastering, finishing a basement, constructing an outdoor tool shed, concrete work, landscaping, and electrical work. This does not include such routine tasks as yard maintenance, heavy housecleaning, minor plumbing repairs, fixing cracked concrete, and so on. They can do as much, if not more, physical labor in one day as we can; moreover, they have handyman skills we are likely never to have learned. We are routinely told similar stories by many of our friends and colleagues about their 70-year-old parents. The one problem we middle-aged adults most face is that living hundreds or thousands of miles from our parents means we can't get enough help from them. Often they are too independent to be at our beck and call.

This personal story serves to bolster and introduce the facts we uncovered as we probed the subject of aging across America. We found that old folks are just like the rest of us; they do not conform to any of the widely held, but incorrect, stereotypes associated with growing old. With the help of these 1,575 typical elderly Americans, we can now understand rather more precisely what it means to grow old.

Living arrangements. Throughout the survey we tried whenever possible to talk with the head of the family or household. For married couples, this typically meant the husband. Those who are single or widowed were chiefly women. Although a high incidence of widowed persons live alone (about one-third), the majority of aged are married and live with their spouses. Orangeburg County, which is typical of the rural South, is a bit different: There nearly a tenth of the elderly live apart from their spouse, unofficially separated, despite the fact that they are married.

Two simple statistics on the elderly differentiate them from middle-aged persons: First, only about 5 percent have remained single for their entire lives. For this group of Americans, born between 1880 and 1910, marriage was a universal norm. Second, and even more striking, only 2 percent, or one in fifty, are either divorced or separated, a statistic that holds true even in California. Approximately one million Americans underwent divorce last year, but the elderly among them were negligible. Marriage is still a popular institution, though not quite so stable or durable as in past years. "Till death do us part," the conclusion of the marriage vow, aptly fits older America. It may become outmoded or obsolete in the twenty-first century, as traditional family patterns yield to a growing trend of short-lived marriages, unmarried couples living together, a single status free of stigma, and even communal arrangements, but in 1980 only the loss of a spouse through death terminates marriage for most older Americans.

The subject of living arrangements provides an opportune moment to anticipate a major theme of Part Three—what to do or not to do for the elderly. Some government decisions that try to meet the legitimate needs of older people may be wholly inappropriate twenty, thirty, or forty years from now, and vice versa. Marital counseling is irrelevant in 1980 but may be a crying concern in 2010.

What is worrisome to some, and to those who think about budgets and taxes, is that older people as a group may become more demanding as the years go by. The current generation of elderly grew up when individuals were expected to look after their own affairs. The next generation will have been nurtured under the American version of the welfare state, have taken government benefits for granted, and witnessed the successes of the civil rights and women's movements. They are likely to intensify political pressures for even greater efforts on behalf of aging, even though the great majority of aged will be better off than ever before.

Social relations. As we have seen, the majority of aged homeowners live with their wives and husbands, or with a child and perhaps other non-relatives. Across the wide variety of living experience captured in the seven sites, only 30 percent are alone. But it is extremely important not to equate living alone with physical or social isolation.

There is overwhelming evidence that contemporary society, with its emphasis on the nuclear family, has not isolated old folks. Most still live near their children and grandchildren and visit frequently, despite the fact that in our highly mobile society nearly one family in five moves each year. Studies conducted in the 1960s disclosed that 80 to 90 percent of the elderly lived within one hour's travel of their nearest child. Among them, nearly 40 percent saw their children daily, and another 40 percent did so at least once a week.

The 1974 Harris survey reaffirmed these earlier findings. Of all those questioned with living children, over half said they had seen them within the last day or so; 80 percent within the last week. We found the same pattern in our more focused survey of elderly homeowners: About 80 percent have one or more relatives either in the same city (or county) or within two hours of traveling time. This is true in every region, climate, and urban or rural area. It is true for blacks and whites. It holds for rich and poor alike. Only a small minority of the elderly are truly on their own.

Nor do old people withdraw from social or community activities upon retirement. Over half of our homeowners belong to one or more social groups—church-related, veterans, and fraternal—and fully 20 percent freely give of their time in unpaid volunteer work. Because the subject of social isolation has received so much publicity, we specifically asked the question "Have you felt more isolated from society as you have grown older?" About three-quarters replied no.

Old folks today are quite adamant about maintaining their independence. The occasional story of an outcast elderly man or woman grossly distorts the truth, which is that most elderly prefer to be on their own. Given the choice, the different generations of an extended family prefer living apart from each other. Most elderly want love and attention from their children, but not necessarily their help with money, housing, or other charitable gestures. Indeed, some prefer to do things for their children and grandchildren, rather than be on the receiving end of things.

Besides helping fix things around their children's house, older people often do such things for their children and grandchildren as give gifts, help them out when someone is ill, take care of grandchildren, help out with money, shop, run errands, and offer advice on a whole range of questions that touch family, home, or business. Nor does this pattern of activity decline with advancing age: Those over 80 are nearly as active as those between 65 and 80. Except for helping out with money or giving gifts, the poor are just as active as the wealthy, especially when it comes to home maintenance. The things old people do for their children are worth a good deal of money, both in time and cash.

Economic status. It is a common theme among writers on aging that old age is synonymous with poverty, that retirement is a stepping-down from the middle class into poverty. Dr. Robert N. Butler, director of the National Institute on Aging, typifies this viewpoint. His book *Why Survive? Being Old in America* devotes a chapter to the subject "How to Grow Old and Poor in an Affluent Society." In one of the leading textbooks in the field of social gerontology, *The Social Forces in Later Life*, Professor Robert Atchley states that the single most demoralizing fact of life for most older people is that they are poor. Much of the academic and the popular press concur in their claims about the impoverished aged.

Yet a more careful assessment of the economic well-being of the elderly presents a somewhat different picture. While survey evidence suggests that a majority of the aged may have current incomes below the poverty line, there are at least three sources of inflation in this figure. First, both scholars and the Census Bureau recognize a tendency among survey respondents to *underreport* their income by a factor of 20 percent or more. A 1968 Social Security Survey (published in 1975) also noted that one-fifth of the surveyed elderly did not provide sufficient information from all sources to permit the computation of total money income. Income from assets was even less well reported.

A second source of distortion in the estimates of poverty among the aged is the failure to include the cash transfers and in-kind income that the government provides the elderly. The third unmeasured source of economic well-being is the assets that the elderly have accumulated over their lifetimes, including equity in their homes. When these three factors are taken into account, the economic status of the aged is much more encouraging.

It is helpful to take a closer look at some figures to sort out these issues. Professor James H. Schulz of Brandeis University has pulled together several major reports that set forth the economic facts of America's elderly population. In 1967, the Social Security Administration reported that older Americans received about $60 billion in money income that year, an amount equal to about 10 percent of the nation's total personal income. Bear in mind that the elderly constitute about 10 percent of the total population. A more recent Census Bureau study estimated that the aged received $95.2 billion in 1973, which made up 11.2 percent of total household money income. When these numbers are adjusted to show the effects of subtracting out taxes and adding in the benefits of a number of money transfers—old-age, survivors, and disability insurance; unemployment and workmen's compensation; public and general assistance (welfare); veterans' benefits; and military retired pay—the percentage of total income held by the elderly rises to nearly 14 percent, well in excess of their proportion in the population.

The Census Bureau survey of American family income also found that 77 percent of aged families had incomes of more than $4,000, with single individuals receiving considerably less. Among those who are still employed, nearly half had incomes exceeding $8,000. Nor do these dollar averages include such government in-kind benefits as Medicare and Medicaid, housing subsidies, food stamps, state services and information provided under the Older Americans Act, the national nutrition program for the elderly, Operation Mainstream (old worker manpower programs), Veterans Administration services, and a bevy of private programs.

A whole new set of benefits was put into place in 1974 with the Supplemental Security Income program (SSI). Mollie Orshansky, the originator of the government's poverty index, believes that the SSI payment schedule may be large enough to create some new independent one- and two-person elderly households among those who otherwise would have lost their independence on turning 65. Indeed, the financial situation of elderly Americans improved so dramatically between 1966 and 1977 that poverty among the aged has declined precipitously. Using data collected in 1965 and 1966, Marilyn Moon calculated that the inclusion of eleven kinds of government transfers reduced the incidence of families beneath the poverty line from more than 30 to only 14 percent when in-kind benefits are counted.

But the level of incomes and government benefits have not remained static. By 1973, money incomes alone for the elderly kept all but 16 percent of them out of poverty. Again, the inclusion of other government transfers (besides Social

49

Security) and in-kind benefits further improves the picture. In June 1977 the Congressional Budget Office released an estimate of elderly family income that included both money transfers and the value of government in-kind benefits, notably Medicare and Medicaid. Among the sixteen million elderly families (including one-person households) in America, only 6 percent have an after-tax, after-transfer income below the poverty level. Less than one million elderly households quality as poverty stricken, virtually the same number as are institutionalized. These facts on income bear little resemblance to the repeated claims of growing impoverishment.

An emphasis on income figures and government transfers tells only a portion of the financial story; most elderly also have some assets. Among homeowners, the lion's share of these assets consists chiefly of the equity in their homes, which has increased substantially in the past seven years. Bear in mind that most older people have no mortgage payments to meet. In the last chapter we shall discuss the subject of reverse annuities, that is, how elderly homeowners can convert their home equity into a regular flow of extra income.

Finally, older people receive a number of special tax benefits and other discounts. These include no sales tax on prescription drugs, a double personal exemption on federal income tax returns, special treatment of retirement income, no tax on up to $100,000 of gains realized from the sale of a home (which superseded the previous exclusion of $35,000), payments to grandparents for the care of their grandchildren eligible for the child-care tax credit, senior citizens discounts for bus fares and movie tickets, free checking accounts, and so on. All of these benefits save the elderly several billion dollars in taxes and fees.

These facts on income contradict the image of poverty. On the same subject, the 1974 Harris poll showed how the images and reality of old age clash. For example, three-fifths of all elderly respondents felt that "most people over 65" face a serious shortage of funds. When asked if this problem applies personally, only one in seven says he or she doesn't have enough money.

How do our sampled elderly fare against these income figures? In order to attain a comprehensive picture of their total money income, we included all questions about income from the University of Michigan's Survey of Consumer Finance: wages and salary, professional fees, farming, dividends, Social Security, Supplemental Security Income, other government grants, pensions, income from rental property, alimony, income from family, and all other income. Remember that people are reluctant to disclose their full income. We encountered some of this reluctance: Only 1,084 of our 1,575 elderly homeowners answered all questions on income. For these respondents, average income from all sources in 1974 exceeded $7,700. However, the distribution of this income is not uniform among sites: Only 10 percent received less than $2,500 in Philadelphia compared with 53 percent in Orangeburg County.

Efforts to reconstruct total assets met with an expected lower response rate: Only 579 elderly homeowners (about 37 percent) willingly gave information about all of the following: certificates of deposit, savings accounts, checking accounts, common stock, mutual funds, investment club stocks, United States savings bonds, other bonds, real estate property, and life insurance. Excluding house equity, over half of the 579 respondents have less than $5,000 in assets; about one-third have more than $10,000. Again, the distribution is not uniform: Excluding Orangeburg County, only 11 percent in the other six sites have no assets. The corresponding figure in Orangeburg is 61 percent. Although assets of homeowners average $18,700 overall, they range from a low of $2,600 in Orangeburg to a high of $32,260 in San Francisco.

Over 80 percent of the elderly we surveyed own their

homes free and clear. For them, and the others we sampled, home equity is the major form of wealth. On average, it comprised $25,630 per respondent. Those in the San Francisco SMSA had the highest average ($38,370) and those in Orangeburg County the lowest ($13,480).

Economists have recently begun to try to define and estimate the overall economic well-being of the elderly. Some have argued that workers build up assets through savings and investment during their working years in anticipation of their use for consumption purposes during retirement years. In her book on this subject, Professor Marilyn Moon analyzes the theoretical issues associated with the specification and measurement of the present income value of elderly-owned assets. Although her information was more comprehensive than what we obtained in our survey, it is nonetheless very revealing to generate a rough estimate of the income potential of our elderly homeowners.

Our calculations rest on several simplifying assumptions. First, we assumed the value of unspent assets would rise with inflation. Savings accounts typically increase at a rate slower than inflation, but home values have outpaced inflation. Second, we assumed that the elderly would want to spend their assets in roughly equal yearly amounts for the balance of their lives. Finally, to be conservative about the income requirements produced by their longevity, we estimated their expected remaining lifetimes as one and one-half times the average length of life for those of similar age and sex.

With these assumptions, and the information collected on the value of each family's assets (including home equity), we calculated for each family a yearly annuity that could be added to current income. The average annuity ranged from a high of $4,440 in San Francisco to a low of $780 in Orangeburg. When these numbers are added to current income, we can derive a rough approximation of the potential yearly income of each homeowner during the survey period.

Excepting Orangeburg County, those sampled in each site averaged over $7,500 in potential income. Again, San Francisco ranked first with $14,630 and those in Orangeburg County last at $4,030.

These numbers can be compared with the government's poverty line. For each site, we computed the percentage of homeowners with total potential incomes below this line. Overall, only 11 percent fell below the poverty line. Only in Orangeburg County was there a high incidence of poverty with the annuity correction—nearly 40 percent.

In our survey, as in most others, respondents tend to refuse to answer at least one, and sometimes several, questions about their income and wealth. Were our calculations of potential income and poverty sensitive to willingness to answer all questions about financial status? To test for possible bias in our results, we recalculated all figures for those who had no more than one refusal on the income and wealth questions (59 percent of our sample) and again for those who had no more than two (74 percent). The results are virtually unchanged. For both recalculations, only 11 percent of our respondents can be classified as poor. In no case did the percentage of poor at an individual site vary by more than 4 percent among the three estimates.

We are confident that these estimates of the economic well-being of the elderly are reliable. Note also that we have not included the value of in-kind benefits (e.g., Medicare and food stamps) that our respondents may perhaps enjoy. Nor did we correct for underreporting of income and wealth that may have occurred in the survey.

In sum, our best estimate is that, outside of the one rural area we sampled, about one-tenth of elderly homeowners are truly poor. This is a far cry from the impression created in the popular press and in many academic works. Orangeburg County has a significant element of poverty, and other studies concur that poverty among the elderly is disproportionately high in rural areas. However, less than a third of all elderly live in rural areas. Our analysis therefore suggests that the vast majority of elderly homeowners enjoy an adequate level of economic well-being.

Health and physical well-being. Recall that some 4 to 5 percent of old folks live in nursing homes and other institutions; these are the truly ill and physically incapacitated. Most elderly homeowners are in satisfactory health. Satisfactory health does not mean the same thing as the absence of serious health ailments, but it does mean the self-perception of good health and the ability to continue an independent life in one's own home. It may be helpful to elaborate this point.

Many older Americans have one or more specific health problems that accompany old age, yet they do not regard these as signs of ill health. Typical illnesses include ulcers, back and leg problems, heart disease, respiratory difficulties (bronchitis, emphysema, asthma), arthritis and rheumatism, and hearing, speech, and vision loss. A study of inner-city elderly residents of a major city in upstate New York found that three-quarters of all elderly residents questioned cited one or more of these specific health problems. However, when asked to rate their health as either excellent, good, fair, or poor, only about 10 per cent claimed poor health. Mental attitude is clearly as important as actual medical condition so far as an older person's view of his or her health is concerned.

It came as no surprise, then, that most elderly homeowners think they are in good health. Although 60 percent of our sample claim one or more current health problems (from a low of 56 percent in New Ulm to a high of 69 percent in Orangeburg), only 12 percent describe their state of health as "poor." If we eliminate Orangeburg residents from this calculation, the percentage in poor health falls to 8. To focus on the one-eighth in ill health is to gloss over the seven-eighths for whom ill health is not a serious problem. Even those who told our interviewers they were in poor health said they encountered little difficulty getting medical assistance when needed.

The 1974 Harris survey is similarly encouraging. Although half of his elderly respondents think most people over 65 are, in general, affected with poor health, only 21 percent put themselves in that category. Because Harris also interviewed renters, those living with children or relatives, and institutionalized elderly, his percentages are somewhat higher than those found in our homeowner survey. In the same survey, only 10 percent of older Americans said they could not obtain adequate medical care. While certain minorities of older people may not receive adequate medical care, serious health problems are by no means as pervasive as the public thinks.

We have touched on direct medical ailments, but physical mobility and strengths are equally important. Can old folks feed and clothe themselves, clean house, walk up and down stairs, do laundry, go shopping, or change storm windows? Only two tasks pose real problems: 58 percent cannot change storm windows easily (20 percent say they can't do it at all), and a third find it hard to go up and down stairs. But with the exception of changing storm windows, fewer than one in twenty say it is impossible for them to perform these various activities; and those who live in the South and West regions have no storm windows to change. In general, then, an overall perception of good health among old folks is reinforced in their physical ability to care for themselves and their homes.

Education. Before we explore the attitudes old folks hold about aging for others, aging for themselves, and life in their communities, we should briefly note that few persons born at the turn of the century could afford the luxury of a college or university education. Altogether, well under half earned a high school diploma, and only one in five has ever enrolled for university studies. On average, big-city residents are better educated than their small-town or rural brethren. But limited formal education of a half century ago is not the same thing as functional illiteracy: 90 percent of older people say they read a daily newspaper.

Race.   Race and racial differences are explosive subjects, ones on which dispassionate discussion is all too often overwhelmed by emotional outbursts and political agitation. The Bakke case, "affirmative action," housing discrimination, school desegregation, and IQ controversies are just a few examples. Yet there is the realization that the issue cannot be skirted.

The opening paragraph of *The Urban Elderly Poor*, a study of the inner-city aged in upstate New York, accepted this challenge.

> What began as a study of the elderly poor in Rochester's Model Cities area became a study of race relations as well. Both the multiracial character of the inner city and the replies obtained in a survey of the elderly revealed that the issue of race was unquestionably the most salient concern in the daily lives of the aged, especially for the white residents. To overlook the racial dimensions of aging would preclude a comprehensive understanding of the preferences of the elderly poor, their social action potential, and the likelihood that programs designed in their behalf can succeed. And, most important of all, it would omit a consideration of the fact that the conditions of the black and aged white are radically distinct. It means one thing to be a poor, old, white, inner-city resident and yet another to be black.

Sterne and his colleagues found that whites are richer, better educated, live longer, disproportionately own their own homes, have better jobs, retain more stable households, and do not receive welfare. Blacks, on the other hand, are poorer, live in rental and less spacious accommodations, are poorly educated, and depend more heavily on welfare.

Under the inspiration of a black gerontologist at Duke University, Dr. Jacquelyne Johnson Jackson, more and more scholars have addressed the special research needs of black older Americans. Herbert Golden of the New York City Department for the Aging wrote his doctoral dissertation on the black elderly. He concluded that applied research that treats black and white elderly alike cannot solve problems faced by black elderly. For Golden, race is a social reality that must be taken into account whenever one offers policy or planning alternatives. He claims that only when blacks are studied in their own context, rather than in comparison with the larger white elderly population, can their unique problems be attacked.

Golden's plea has not gone unheard. In 1977 the Institute of Gerontology of the University of Michigan published a pamphlet by Joseph Dancy, Jr., entitled *The Black Elderly: A Guide for Practitioners*. Dancy urges all social workers who deal with the elderly to be aware of the particular needs, problems, and strengths of the black elderly— differences that stem from past and present discrimination and their greater poverty. The pamphlet identifies nine predominantly black universities with gerontology training programs and also provides the address and activities of the National Center on Black Aged.

In the September–October 1978 issue of *Aging*, the official bimonthly journal of the Administration on Aging, six authors consumed forty double-column pages on the subject of black aging. These articles focused on black demographics, social policy, special health problems, family roles, federal action, and barriers to adequate housing. The theme that underpinned this issue is that blacks have special problems beyond those of income, decent housing, social services, and good health, which are common to all Americans. These special problems are traceable to their historically limited educational opportunities, which deprived them of better jobs, higher earnings, and more comfortable housing.

Of equal importance, racial discrimination has inflicted psychological and financial costs on elderly blacks.

Approximately six and one-half percent of all elderly homeowners are black. As we reveal in the chapters to follow, their homeowning experience differs significantly from that of whites. In Part Two we look closely at the homes of aged whites and blacks and discover very great disparities in patterns of upkeep. There we offer possible explanations for these facts, but the point remains that they cannot be overlooked or dismissed in any comprehensive treatment of old folks at home.

Attitudes About Aging

Money, health, and family ties make up part of the material things in life. But life also has a non-material dimension, what social psychologists refer to as attitudes. These intangibles are often as important as material possessions. Self-perception of health among older people is far more favorable than a statistical portrait of their serious ailments would suggest. In this section we want to examine this intangible dimension of aging. What do the elderly think about retirement living? How does the reality of old age fit their expectations? What level of self-esteem do they have? Do old folks themselves subscribe to the negative images of aging that society holds? What are their chief fears and worries? Do they like their homes and their neighborhoods? Do they feel content or trapped in their housing? The replies to these and other questions flesh out the financial, physical, and other tangible dimensions of aging thus far described.

Aging in general. Images of old age in the American media too often highlight negative stereotypes of aging. "The old are represented as stubborn and opinionated, confused and forgetful, unproductive and aimless, resistant to change, sexless, and reduced in intelligence." There is an excessive emphasis on physical and mental illness among the old. Not only do these images potentially impair the dignity of the aged, they also present younger people with a distorted model of aging.

The self-image of old folks is entirely at odds with the media's portrayal of aging. Those with whom we talked put forth a very pronounced statement of personal independence and individual responsibility. When asked if "people should take care of themselves all through life," almost 90 percent replied yes. Three-quarters said they viewed the "retirement years as special," another positive affirmation of life. Most elderly (80 percent) also thought that the problems they still face can be resolved by concerted effort on their part—not a reflection of alienation, apathy, or resignation to old age. These optimistic statements go hand in hand with the facts of aging: The vast majority of elderly are financially, medically, physically, and mentally fit.

Louis Harris interviewers attest to the same positive view of aging in America. Across the range of problems they examined—fear of crime, poor health, too little income, loneliness, inadequate medical care, feeling unwanted, not enough to do to keep busy, and so on—the experiences of the aged contradicted the public images of aging. Personal testimony shows that the problems of older people are comparable to those of younger people, even though old and young alike accept a negative image of old age. Harris interprets these results to mean that older people see life as tough, but that they, as individuals, are merely exceptions to this rule. Old folks see themselves as bright, alert, open-minded, and quite capable of getting things done: Their self-esteem is as high as that in the younger population.

For many older people, life has turned out better than they expected it to be. Compared with the 37 percent who say life is better than they expected, only 11 percent say it is worse. The problems many feared in old age never materialized because most old folks have enjoyed adequate income, good health, and long and stable marriages. In general, older people believe that their living conditions have improved in the last two decades. More so than the young, they also feel that today's elderly are better off financially than in the past and represent little economic burden to society.

Overall, the elderly view their own lives as no worse than the young in regard to problems of money, medical care, education, housing, social isolation, and so forth. Although they have smaller incomes, with fewer dependents to support and fewer financial needs overall, the elderly cite fewer financial troubles than the low-income young. Old people are, generally, neither lonely nor isolated, and a majority have no need for senior citizens' centers or golden age clubs. This portrait of aging bears little resemblance to the public image of aging, as portrayed in the media or held among ordinary people.

Feelings about home and neighborhood. It is widely believed that many older people are forcibly overhoused. Forced home ownership, as this argument goes, means that the homes elderly persons purchased thirty years ago in which to raise their families are situated either in older working-class neighborhoods on the fringes of central cities or in the central city itself. These neighborhoods have often been victimized by urban blight, and the value of their homes has not kept pace with the cost of new construction. This means that most elderly cannot afford to exchange their large older homes for a small, modern-equipped suburban house. Moreover, suburban development and shrinking central city populations have forced city authorities to raise the tax burden on those who have not fled, of whom the elderly are a growing share. Not only do old folks pay more in taxes, especially for public schools, which provide them no direct benefits,they do so on houses that are older and less well equipped. Just a few years ago, planning officials in the Department of Housing and Urban Development gave serious thought to policies that would encourage "overhoused" elderly to find smaller lodgings elsewhere, thereby freeing up space for large, younger families. These ideas, while never becoming official policy, indicate broad acceptance of the overhousing thesis.

What do the elderly think of their housing? From the answers we obtained, one would scarcely guess that the housing experts and and elderly were discussing the same subject. With trivial exceptions nearly every elderly homeowner is satisfied with his house, whether it is a row house in Philadelphia, a pastel cottage in San Francisco, an old Cape Cod design in Pittsfield, or a ranch house in Tulsa. Of the 4 percent who say they are dissatisfied, virtually all live in Orangeburg County. Not only are the elderly satisfied with their homes, no more than 7 percent would want to leave their house for a condominium, a multi-story apartment, or a mobile home. As to the overhousing thesis, it is soundly rejected: 72 percent find the size of their present home just right.

Some have suggested that elderly homeowners take in boarders in their unused rooms to help with income or maintenance. In our survey, 10 percent say they have unused rooms in their homes. However, only one-fifth of these—or 2 percent of the entire sample—have any interest in renting these rooms to outsiders. The main reason is that most desire complete privacy. Those who advocate that old folks should take in boarders are out of touch with reality.

It is not surprising that most people like their homes. The elderly, like the rest of us, buy homes they like within the means of their budget. Nearly one-third are the original owners of their present homes and three-fifths have not moved for more than twenty years. Memories of children, husbands, and wives are intermingled with these homes. Home ownership for many elderly is economically attractive, less costly than renting a smaller apartment, or purchasing a higher-priced condominium. Fully 87 percent of our sample own their homes free and clear of a mortgage and thus do not have the financial burden of monthly mortgage payments.

Not only do older Americans like their homes, most also have long-standing ties to their neighborhood, churches, and friends—roots in the community. A look at the survey shows that 88 percent want to stay in the same area; only 7 percent said they would like to leave the city or the general area. An even higher proportion—94 percent—are happy with their neighborhood.

In the larger cities, however, the pitfalls of urban life—blight, crime, fear, racial tension—weigh heavily on the minds of older Americans. It is a fact that many elderly dare not go out at night and are often reluctant to open their doors by day to any stranger. Professor Lee Rainwater of Harvard University has shown that a large proportion of older persons are perfectly satisfied with housing that professionals might consider substandard, so long as it provides security against blatant threats. That is, to live safely in a substandard house is better than to live in a standard house set in an unsafe neighborhood. After examining nearly every study of the preferences of elderly residents, Professor James T. Mathieu concluded that the safety and security of the neighborhood are extremely important. Old people want as their neighbor "the right kind of people," preferably people of the same group or race.

Growing concern with crimes against the elderly has stimulated a congressional investigation and publication of several conference volumes on the subject of elderly crime victimization. Although a number of studies conducted by the Law Enforcement Assistance Administration conclude that the elderly overall are not disproportionately victims of violent crime, the general conclusion masks important differences among population subgroups. Inner-city elderly residents suffer much higher victimization rates than the general elderly population, and, equally significant, crimes against old people are increasing more rapidly than against other age groups. The aged have endured the most rapid increase in many kinds of household crimes (burglary, household larceny, and motor vehicle theft).

One reason that old folks have a statistically lower incidence of victimization is that many are afraid to leave their homes. Few travel outside after sunset in the inner city, and most try to avoid dangerous neighborhoods. Harris also found that fear of crime among the elderly deterred attendance at movies, theaters, and restaurants. This fear of crime is as debilitating as being a victim of crime; its impact on the quality of life is so severe that the Senate Select Committee on Aging devoted an entire chapter to the subject in its report.

To return to our sample of respondents, despite their overall satisfaction with home and neighborhood, many point to this precise concern—personal safety and the rising incidence of crime. It is the most frequently voiced complaint. Between one-quarter to one-third of all elderly homeowners in Philadelphia, San Francisco, and Dayton express this alarm (which is virtually nonexistent in Orangeburg County, New Ulm, and Tulsa). Urban decay, again concentrated in the larger cities, took second place. No other problem received more than a handful of marks.

Several residents of Dayton offered poignant remarks.

Rough people moved in. It is not safe to leave your home.

Robbery and thefts which we never had before the low-income housing came in; now it's just terrible.

Similar comments show up in Philadelphia and San Francisco. In the smaller towns and rural areas, crime, and blight are never mentioned as the facts of neighborhood life. Rural and small-town elderly are less troubled by the concerns that govern big-city life.

Martin Mayer has aptly summarized urban reality, especially for inner-city elderly residents:

> What has provoked the decline in the physical condition of so many neighborhoods is a process of *public* disinvestment—a failure to provide adequate police protection, to keep the streets and sidewalks clean, to preserve the behavioral (let alone academic) standards of the schools, to maintain the roads, to supply adequate public transportation. . . .
>
> If the government in a neighborhood does not perform properly the tasks that only the government can accomplish, the people who live in that area will scramble to leave—and then the "housing problem" in that area becomes insoluble.

Many elderly whites resent and fear black migration into their neighborhoods. As white families with school-age children desert the cities for suburban schools, those whites who remain are increasingly elderly homeowners. The presence of blacks (though not necessarily elderly blacks) alters expectations about neighborhoods and property values. This is a tragic situation for all concerned and one that defies easy resolution. It is nonetheless very real.

In the course of our interviews, old folks freely shared their opinions over a whole range of subjects. Their views on race were perhaps most poignant of all.

In the previously mentioned study of elderly residents in upstate New York, more racial animosity was found among elderly whites than among elderly blacks. We found this to be true in our sample as well. When asked to identify neighborhood problems, white homeowners in Dayton, Philadelphia, and San Francisco offered the following comments:

> Blacks may come in and start others coming in and I don't feel they belong here.
>
> Getting blacks in the neighborhood.
>
> Welfare mother and kids moved in on the corner, and I

think she is a prostitute. Noisy and she lets the lights burn, ruining the house and neighborhood. There is lots of noise and callers at odd hours.

Black kids and streetwalkers in area.

However tragic or disagreeable, neighborhood change, the decline of community ties, and racial conflict in our cities blot an otherwise positive affirmation of life for old folks at home.

PART TWO

At Home

4

How the Elderly
See Their Housing

Housing is the largest single expenditure over the course of
an average family's lifetime. Not only does it provide shelter
and comfort, it is for many the only real source of savings,
often constituting 80 to 90 percent of their total financial
assets. At the same time, home ownership is also a financial
and physical burden. Since most elderly do not want to
move, and few can afford to do so, it is important to compare the benefits and burdens of home ownership. In short,
are the aged well housed? What can or should be done by the
government for the aged?

An Image of Despair

Robert N. Butler, director of the National Institute on
Aging, puts many of the elderly into a bleak house. Excerpts
from his powerful book *Why Survive? Being Old in America*
are moving.

> The housing problems of the aged are much more severe
> than is commonly recognized. Housing consumes one-
> third of the budget of an elderly couple. . . . Those who
> own their own houses face great difficulties maintaining
> them, for the home may be their only equity. They often
> lack money to pay for necessary repairs, services and
> property taxes. Many are forced to give up their homes.

What problems face the elderly homeowner? In a chapter entitled "No Place to Live," Butler points to low equity, utility and maintenance costs, property taxes, age discrimination in the granting of new mortgages, and welfare liens on private property. He assembles, on the one hand, income and asset figures, and, on the other hand, utility bills, maintenance costs, and property tax burdens. Butler assumes that these costs outrace their financial capacity. He writes: "This is catastrophic to anyone living on a fixed income." "How does an older person cope physically with all the ordinary problems of homes—carpenter ants, termites, worn-out switches, clogged drains and downspouts, or flooded basements?" "Thus, although older home owners can live free of rent, they are at a disadvantage if they wish to sell and move elsewhere." Butler charges that "both the federal government and private housing enterprise have failed to provide sufficient reasonably priced housing for the elderly."

It is easy to read books, articles, government reports, and statistics and conclude that the housing condition of the elderly is wretched and steadily growing worse. Butler's writing is typical of this theme, but not unique. However, his important role in national policy on aging warrants special evaluation of his findings and recommendations. On this score, we are troubled by his exposition. Our concerns are twofold. First, are the elderly, in fact, less well housed than younger families and incapable of purchasing and maintaining "decent" housing? Second, do the elderly themselves think their housing is inadequate? Butler and those who share his convictions have not shown that the elderly are especially less well housed. More important, he has forgotten to ask elderly homeowners if they think their housing is not adequate.

This omission is not surprising. Social critics and planners are very much victims of a social-work perspective, which states that clients cannot accurately perceive their own problems. The social worker, professional critic, or analyst thinks that only he or she can diagnose a client's problem. To make matters worse, the social worker sometimes views a client's perception of his situation, especially if it differs from the professional diagnosis, either with disdain or as symptomatic of some problem of which the client himself is ignorant. On this view, planners (and critics) have little to gain from asking the elderly to talk about their problems, since the elderly cannot accurately judge their own circumstances. And, should the elderly reject the bleak portrait others paint of them, they can be accused of being ignorant of their own unfortunate situation. If professional critics say that the financial and physical well-being of elderly homeowners is deteriorating, then it must be so—even if the elderly firmly disagree!

And the elderly do disagree. Not only have several studies recently shown that most older people do not consider themselves in need of social services that planners insist they need, as this chapter unfolds we shall also see that elderly homeowners would not accept the critics' description of their lives and housing.

Is it wrong to heed the views of elderly homeowners? Should we depend solely on the conclusions of the experts? Those questions raise fundamental issues of morality and political life, along with the choice of an appropriate way to study aging. Who has the right to decide what other people need and what is best for them? More concretely, should we consciously seek the views of elderly homeowners in formulating our understanding of the problems they face and any solutions they desire? Or should we impose the planners' and the critics' definitions of their needs and simply measure the extent of those needs with official income, health, education, and other statistics, disregarding, in the process, the views of the elderly themselves? This chapter speaks for the elderly, the next for the experts.

71

An Image of Comfort

Many have asserted that old folks tend to live in old homes and that these older homes are potentially troublesome to their owners. At least the first part of this statement is true. One-third of the elderly homeowners we talked with live in homes built more than fifty years ago. Another third date from 1925 to 1945, with the final third of postwar vintage. In all, the average age of the homes in our sample is forty-five years. Homes in the East are, of course, much older than those in the West: Many homes in Pittsfield and Philadelphia were built in the nineteenth century. In Tulsa and San Francisco (victim of the 1906 quake), pre–World War I homes are scarce.

America is a mobile country. One-fifth of its population moves each year. The exceptions to this uprooting are the elderly, who tend to stay put. Many older persons have lived in the same house for most of their adult lives. In Orangeburg County, for example, two-thirds of the elderly are the original owners of their old homes. Elsewhere, the figure is better than one in three. Overall, 60 percent have not moved in the last two decades. Younger people come and go, neighborhoods change, but most elderly homeowners remain.

Recall the problems of elderly owners (as the critics enumerate them). Low equity means that the elderly are trapped in their homes and neighborhoods—they cannot afford to move to a more suitable home and neighborhood in the suburbs. Rising utility and maintenance costs are tragic for those who must survive on limited, fixed incomes. Property taxes eat up a growing share of an elderly family's income. It is tough for old people to get a mortgage if they want to buy a more expensive house. Finally, some states require that old people sign over their homes to the state welfare departments before they can get Supplemental Security Income; this deters old people from applying for public assistance because they do not want to lose control of their property.

How real are these problems? First, less than one in ten want to sell their homes and move to a new type of housing; what they do want is security in the neighborhood they've got. As we show below, most are overwhelmingly satisfied with their homes, even if the fixtures are not the most up-to-date. Second, rising utility and maintenance costs are partially offset by increases in Social Security payments. We should not underestimate the financial impact of skyrocketing utility costs, but as we explained in the last chapter, we should also not underestimate the capacity of the elderly to meet those costs. As well, their homes do not suffer the physical abuse that only growing children can inflict on a house. They also have more time to do minor work on their homes because they no longer have to punch a time clock at work.

Third, property tax is a burden on elderly homeowners, but homestead exemptions and circuit-breaker provisions in state tax laws help ease this burden. By 1974 every state had enacted some type of program to relieve the burden of low-income households, especially the elderly. In California, homeowners who have reached 62 years of age can now postpone their property taxes as long as they wish, on condition that the state will have liens on the homes in order to collect the amount due on their death. The only limitations are that income may not exceed $20,000 a year and that equity in the home must be at least 20 percent of assessed value. Signed into law on October 2, 1977, this bill ensures that California's elderly will not be forced out of their homes by large increases in property values. Thus, rising property taxes harm middle-income families more than elderly households.

Fourth, the problem that the elderly cannot get a mortgage is more apparent than real. Few need to borrow money for their homes, for most own their homes free and clear. Finally, welfare liens affect only a few of the elderly in a handful of Southern states, which can remedy this ill with new legislation.

A new development has radically changed the economic situation for older Americans. Since October 1977, age discrimination in employment became illegal in California. No individual can be forcibly retired at age 65. A national law was enacted in 1978 and takes full effect in 1980. Thus, few elderly need suffer mandatory retirement before 70 at the earliest. The future holds much more attractive income prospects for many elderly homeowners, and a corresponding reduction in financial worries.

The critics' views make for passionate reading and politics but fit a minority of homeowners, and only a small minority at that. It is revealing to let elderly homeowners do their own talking. Only they can say if their homes and neighborhoods are comfortable and safe for them, and if home ownership is a painfully growing burden.

How Old Folks See Their Housing

Let's construct a model home for the typical older American family based on our survey. The average aged family inhabits a six- to seven-room house, which provides nearly twice as much space per person as the homes of younger families: Older families are almost never over-crowded. Apart from the rural areas, virtually every house has an indoor toilet. Ninety-nine homes in one hundred have adequate kitchen facilities that include working stoves and refrigerators. The typical home has a living room, dining room, kitchen, bathroom, and three bedrooms. Ranch homes in Tulsa and pastel cottages in San Francisco reflect regional taste and modern design. The multi-story row house in Philadelphia reflects an older style of housing.

Anyone who has lived in the same house for more than

twenty years is likely to know the ins and outs of his or her home. We set about to capture those impressions in a systematic way that would result in a set of reliable, unbiased answers. Asking old folks to evaluate their homes, item by item, would help establish the accuracy of the critics' assertions about them. To insure that our interviewers did not prompt or prejudice the replies of our elderly homeowners, we phrased our questions most carefully. To us, the most innocuous wording in any question we might ask was the notion of *adequacy.* "Is your refrigerator adequate?" A "yes" answer means that the refrigerator provides useful and satisfactory storage of foodstuffs to its owner. A "no" answer might signal that the refrigerator was too small, not dependable, or unsatisfactory in some other manner.

A refrigerator can provide adequate service yet still need some repair. We thus asked a second question of each owner: "Does your refrigerator need repair?" On the second query, the respondent will have had a chance to think about a subject that might not have occurred to him or her before. So it would not be surprising that a succession of questions that asked about the condition of, say, a kitchen appliance, would find that each successive asking yielded a higher incidence of problems or defects.

Each homeowner was first asked to evaluate the overall condition of his or her home in very general terms and to give his or her own reasons why any portion of the home might be unsatisfactory.

Now I would like to talk about your house in more detail.

- Is the plumbing in this house adequate?
  (If no) In what ways is the plumbing inadequate?
- Is the electrical system—that is, the lighting, wiring, and outlets—in this house adequate?
- Is the heating system in this house adequate?
- Are the roof and gutter systems adequate in this house?

- Are the basic structure and foundation—that is, the floors, walls, stairways—adequate in this house?
- Is the exterior of your house—that is, the outside walls, walkways, windows—adequate in this house?
- What about the kitchen appliances—such as the stove and the refrigerator—are they adequate in this house?

The questioning then moved from this very broad level to a specific recounting of twenty-eight separate aspects of each house. The questioning went as follows:

Now I'd like to run through a list of specific household features. Please tell me if any of these need some repair or maintenance work.

- How about your hot water heater—do you feel it needs repair or maintenance work?
    (If yes) Is it or will it be a very serious problem if it doesn't get repaired?
        (If yes) Are you going to repair it soon?
        What are your plans for repair?
        What do you think it will cost?

If the homeowner said that he or she did not plan to fix a housing element that needed serious repair, we asked, "Why aren't you going to repair it?" These questions let each elderly person identify which items he thinks need repair, if it is a serious problem, and whether he could or could not make these repairs. Altogether, we reviewed with each owner the following list of housing features:

- toilets
- washbasins
- tubs and/or showers
- fuse box
- light fixtures
- light switches
- electrical outlets

- furnace
- furnace thermostat
- radiators or heat registers
- gutters
- shingles or other roof surface
- deck of roof
- floors
- ceilings
- walls
- staircases
- foundation
- outside walls
- windows
- screens or storm windows
- outside stairs and walkways
- outside doors
- oven
- kitchen sink
- stove
- refrigerator

Taken together, these two sets of questions embody a very thorough personal assessment of each family's housing. The first set talks in very general terms and the second in highly specific and concrete terms.

How then do old folks see their homes? The results to the first set of questions are overwhelming: Almost every homeowner sees each part of his home as adequate. Only in Orangeburg County, in the rural South, did percentages fall below 90. Even there, fully two-thirds or more said each part of their home was adequate. The incidence of inadequacy in the rural population is three to five times as great as in urban areas, but this comes as no surprise since rural incomes are lower, and 90 percent of all homes without flush toilets are located in rural areas.

These percentages indicate whether homeowners see in-

HOUSE FEATURE	PERCENT ADEQUATE
Plumbing	94%
Electrical	96
Heating	97
Roof & gutters	88
Structure & foundation	95
House exterior	90
Kitchen appliances	96

adequacies in each feature of their homes, taken one at a time. Although some owners may report a problem in only one housing dimension, others may see two, three, all the way up to seven inadequacies. We want to know, then, how many elderly see no problems at all throughout their entire house, and how many see multiple problems. These calculations reveal that 77 percent of the 1,575 respondents regard their homes as trouble free; of the remaining 23 percent, better than half report only one problem. Overall, only one in ten have multiple housing problems.

These findings bear repeating. From the standpoint of the elderly homeowner, most dwellings adequately meet their residents' needs. Again, from this standpoint, the nation's elderly-owned housing stock does not suffer widespread decay. Elderly homeowners are, in all likelihood, better housed than they have ever been before.

What happened as we moved to a breakdown of twenty-eight separate housing features that allowed each respondent to assess the condition of his house in far greater detail? As before, the answers demonstrate that most homes serve their owners well.

These summary numbers mask important differences between areas. Orangeburg County residents say that two to three times as many specific things in their homes need repair as their urban counterparts.

As before, some owners cite only one feature in need of

How the Elderly See their Housing

House Feature	Percent Needing Repair
Water heater	3%
Toilets	5
Wash basins	4
Tubs/showers	3
Fusebox	2
Light fixtures	3
Light switches	3
Electrical outlets	4
Furnace	3
Thermostat	2
Radiator	1
Gutters	8
Roof surface	15
Roof deck	4
Floors	6
Ceilings	8
Walls	7
Staircases	1
Foundation	5
Outside walls	12
Windows	13
Screens/storm windows	9
Outside walks	6
Outside doors	7
Oven	5
Kitchen sink	3
Stove	5
Refrigerator	4

repair; others identify two or more. It is useful, then, to know how many believe all twenty-eight features are in good working order, how many think only one needs repair, two, three, and so on.

Focusing on the urban locations, in which most elderly owners live, over half cannot find a single household feature that needs repair. Another fifth say that only one of the twenty-eight items needs repair. Elderly in the rural site are not so fortunate. Over half cite at least two items in need of repair.

NUMBER OF FEATURES THAT NEED REPAIR	URBAN (SIX SITES)	RURAL (ONE SITE)
None	55%	29%
One	20	14
Two or more	25	57

Are these repairs of a serious nature? Each older person was asked to judge the seriousness of any problem he or she identified and to state why he or she might not make the repair. Between a third to a half of the needed repairs were regarded as serious. In all, only 22 percent have a serious problem that needs repair. Of these—and this result is most important—only one in eight, or just about 3 percent of the entire sample, say they would not make what they regard as a needed repair because of a lack of money; virtually none cite health as a reason. In other words, only three in every one hundred elderly homeowners say that they don't have enough money to repair a serious problem. This picture is hardly one either of massive deterioration or widespread impoverishment.

To summarize, only about one-fourth of the elderly say they have either a general inadequacy in their home or some specific element that is in serious need of repair. Three-fourths, the great majority, of elderly homeowners we sampled see no serious problems in their house; and of those who do, only a trivial few say they can't afford to fix their homes. If we are to believe the views of the elderly themselves, there seems to be no specific crisis of housing.

To anticipate Part Three of this book, these findings raise the issue of how best we might help old folks who can't afford to fix their homes—what is often called the targeting problem in delivering services to needy people. It will not do simply to locate those persons who report problems of repair (itself a costly activity) and offer financial assistance, since few of them identify lack of money as the reason for disrepair. In this case, throwing money at the problem will definitely not solve it. It may be necessary for us to accept the reality of elderly homeowners, which is a willingness on their part to live in an imperfect home.

How Old Folks Cope with Home Maintenance

"How does an older person cope physically with all the ordinary problems of homes—carpenter ants, termites, wornout switches, clogged drains and downspouts, or flooded basements?" Butler implies, with this question, that older persons do not and cannot easily cope. We suspect this question was purely rhetorical, with an implicit negative answer. However, letting elderly homeowners talk for themselves casts doubt on this view. Not only do old folks cope with ordinary maintenance problems, in all likelihood they do so more effectively then their children or other younger American families. After all, they have experienced home ownership for the better part of their adult lives, and have demonstrably run their households successfully for decades.

At one time or another, most people remodel or add a room onto their homes; nearly half of all elderly homeowners we interviewed have either remodeled, made additions, or contracted for major construction work since acquiring their homes. Thus, many have had experience dealing with contractors and large-scale do-it-yourself housing projects. However, major work is infrequently done, especially after retirement, and it is often contracted to professional firms.

Each homeowner was asked to list every repair he completed in the past two years and how much money he spent on that work. About one-fifth of the elderly spent $500 or more on household repairs, whereas over half spent no money at all. The average household annual expenditure for repairs and maintenance comes to about $187, which is only a small percentage of total household income. Since 80 percent of elderly homeowners have no mortgage payments to meet, the cost of home repairs and maintenance may be less a burden to old people than to younger families.

When an elderly homeowner has a problem that he cannot fix himself, on whom does he rely for assistance? Where does he get information about potential contractors?

It turns out that a majority (about 54 percent) rely either entirely upon themselves or on an immediate relative to correct a house problem. Small numbers ask their neighbors or friends outside the neighborhood. Of those who told us they had done some work on their house in the past two years, about equal numbers depended on themselves and friends as on employed professional help.

Are elderly homeowners at the mercy of unscrupulous contractors? It would not seem so. Ninety-four percent of the 400-odd homeowners who have recently employed a contractor expressed satisfaction with the quality of the work. Overall, 90 percent of our sample described local repair work service in favorable terms. There may be some instances of unscrupulous contractor behavior, but this is not the aggregate reality of the elderly homeowner.

In the course of talking with elderly homeowners, we also interviewed contracting firms in each community to compare their services and costs with the homeowners' concepts of their activities and prices. Accordingly, we tried systematically to interview eighteen companies in each site. Telephone directories were consulted in each community to compile a list of companies; these lists were complemented with a search of newspaper advertisements and government records to prepare a complete roster of contractors including small independent operators. In all but two sites, we successfully interviewed eighteen contractors. In New Ulm only fifteen contractors are in business, and all fifteen were interviewed. In rural Orangeburg County only three firms were contacted. All told, then, we assembled evidence (through the use of a prestructed questionnaire) on 108 companies selling repair services.

The portrait of community repair services conforms to our everyday expectations. It is a heterogeneous collection of multi-service firms. A majority of firms typically engage in such broad services as new construction, renovation, remodeling, and additions, as well as repairs and maintenance services; only one in four specializes in new building. Some firms try to specialize in work on such specific housing problems as roofs, plumbing, heating, painting, electricity, floors, siding, and foundation work. But the overall image is one of multi-purpose repair services available in each of the several communities, with specialized services available if desired.

Do sellers of repair services encounter any specific difficulties in working for elderly homeowners? Do they ever refuse jobs from elderly homeowners? Overall, contractors view the elderly in much the same light as homeowners of all ages. In response to the question "Have you ever consciously refused to do work for elderly people?" *all* respondents replied no. Only 13 percent of the surveyed firms have never done work for elderly persons, but these did not reflect conscious refusal. Approximately 8 per cent say it costs more to do work for elderly people. Nearly 14 percent report they have encountered particular difficulties working for elderly people, which ranged from problems of job loan finance, to old-fashioned ideas about material and unnecessary supervision. Also included is the time required to obtain their confidence since many do not understand the importance of original contracts. Finally, several contractors claim that some elderly persons take too long to make a decision on repair work. But after reciting these difficulties in services performed for the elderly, no contractor expressed a reluctance to do work for aged homeowners. By and large, sellers of repair services treat elderly homeowners no different from their younger counterparts. This result is virtually identical with the prior statement that elderly homeowners are satisfied with contractors they have used. If unscrupulous contractors exist, they evidently do not enjoy their ill-earned profits at the disproportionate expense of the elderly.

We have emphasized in this chapter the importance of understanding the views that the elderly themselves put forth, of what they consider personally important as they evaluate the quality and condition of their homes. By focusing on the views of the elderly, we avoid the imputation of our own norms and standards, or those of some specialist group of experts, who may stand to gain from imposing an artificially high standard. Letting the elderly talk for themselves generates a startling but encouraging result: The vast majority of elderly do not consider their homes to need significant repairs or maintenance work.

5

The Experts' View

IN 1949, THE United States Congress passed a National Housing Act that set forth the goal of "a decent home in a suitable living environment" for every American family. The motives underlying this congressional declaration are surely praiseworthy. However, Congress never defined "decent" or a "suitable living environment." Unless these words can be defined in practical terms, how can we judge to what extent the goals espoused in the 1949 Housing Act have been met?

The idea of a decent home implies that we can determine, in some reasonable manner, a standard beneath which a house is surely considered to be inadequate. Yet even this determination is not a straightforward task. Standards do not remain fixed in time and space. Rising incomes and rising social expectations tend to raise minimum standards. Each success in improving the quality and condition of housing in America has stimulated the establishment of new and higher standards. Moreover, standards differ across national, regional, or cultural boundaries: Nathan Glazer has argued that housing conditions that are quite acceptable to most families in Mexico and Hong Kong, and which do not have any clear negative impact for those families, would be in violation of even the most minimal standards in the United States and would, in the minds of most middle-class Americans, be associated with chaos in family life.

Despite the ambiguities, uncertainties, and frequent changes in the interpretation of a "decent" home, analysts have traditionally focused on three facets of housing: quality and condition of housing, overcrowding, and ability to pay for housing. If a home is in very bad condition or lacks plumbing facilities, it is regarded as substandard. If a family is overcrowded or is forced to pay too high a share of its income for housing, these conditions signify a serious problem. The definition and measures of bad condition, overcrowding, and unreasonable housing costs constitute an interesting history of the social meaning of substandard housing and the size of the apparent housing problem.

The Definition of Housing

What exactly is housing? How do we know which facets of a home to examine to determine if it is substandard? The answers to these questions are largely influenced by social, economic, and political premises. The desirable characteristics of a house are different things to different people. For some, a spacious backyard is a necessity for playful children; for others, it is an intolerable maintenance burden. Some relish the open spaces of country living; others abhor commuting and wish to live close to downtown for the convenience it brings. Some regard a multi-story residence as inherently unsafe; others find a ranch home aesthetically unlivable. From these examples it is clear that the concept of an ideal house is impossible. However, despite differences in the desirability of neighborhood surroundings, location, and environment of a house, it might be possible to agree that each house should have such basic facilities as a bathroom, internal water supply, kitchen, electricity, and so on.

Even with a consensus on basic facilities, the quality of a house is still largely determined by what we can afford. In the United States, as in other countries, each homeowner buys as close to a reasonable approximation of his "ideal" house as his budget permits. The American ideal house is more luxurious than that found overseas because Americans have more money to spend for housing. Indeed, because people in other countries can only afford lesser amounts of housing, it makes little sense to adopt standards for international comparison.

Not only is it impossible for us to agree upon the ideal house, even professional housing analysts disagree on what the terms "housing" and "housing services" mean. Professor Wallace Smith of the University of California insists that housing is much more complex than merely shelter: Bound up with the concept of housing are the dimensions of privacy (that is, separate shelter), location, environmental amenities (e.g., quality and prestige of the local schools, such urban services as parks, playgrounds, hospitals, and the class of people in the neighborhood), and the fact that for many Americans housing is an investment as well as a place to live. Housing, in this view, is a very special economic commodity: unlike conventional goods and services, it is very durable, is of high cost, is virtually immobile, and carries with it the strong emotional mystique of homeownership.

Others find this characterization too limited. In a book published by the Center for Urban Policy Research at Rutgers University, William Grigsby and Louis Rosenburg enumerate many more separate dimensions of housing that potentially harm poor people: lack of adequate housing space, quality, and furnishings; poor neighborhood environment; excessive housing costs relative to family income; lack of security of occupancy; restrictions upon choice of tenure; restricted locational choice; lack of special housing services for the physically handicapped; racial discrimination; excessive housing cost relative to quality and quantity of space received; and the stigma attached to receiving housing assistance.

Housing Standards

Substandard housing, like beauty, is in the eye of the beholder; it takes on a wide variety of interpretations and yields conflicting estimates of the national housing problem.

We have no immediate solution to this thorny conceptual issue. Rather, what we can and will do is review the historical application of the major measures of housing standards in America and distill some general trends either of housing improvement or deterioration. On the basis of this distillation of standards and measures of housing adequacy, the quality and condition of America's elderly-owned homes will be analyzed.

Quality and condition. The first and certainly most talked about measure of standards is that of quality or condition of both the interior and exterior of a house. Two different approaches govern most discussion of substandard housing. The first is the social-hygiene approach whose underlying premise states that unfit housing gives rise to ill health or threatens personal safety. To eliminate substandard housing, in this view, is thus to remove from the housing environment all impediments to health and safety. The second approach to housing standards is monetary: How much does it cost to correct the substandard features of a house? We first review a set of attempts to measure housing quality that reflect the social-hygiene approach.

Early private concern with poor housing conditions dates back to charitable movements in the mid-nineteenth century. In 1844 the New York Association for Improving the Condition of the Poor surveyed cellar tenements and "branded the housing of the poor as morally debasing and, because of high rents, economically oppressive." Efforts to measure the structural quality and condition of housing have been constantly altered in search of better and better measures. The first national housing data on physical quality and conditions was collected by the Real Property Inventories program in the 1930s in a public works project to combat the Depression. In 1940, for the first time, the Census Bureau asked a similar set of questions about housing. Census takers were instructed to observe each housing unit in the field and give it a rating of Good Condition, Needs Minor Repair, Needs Major Repair, and Unfit for Use. If a home was classified as needing major repairs or unfit for use, and if it lacked separate bathing and toilet facilities or an internal supply of running water, it was declared substandard.

The Census Bureau was not entirely happy with its 1940 classifications. The limited distinction between homes "needing major repairs" and "not needing major repairs" was therefore replaced in the 1950 census with a conceptual distinction between "dilapidated" and "not dilapidated"; in turn, the bureau switched in the 1960 census to a three-way classification of "sound," "deteriorating," and "dilapidated." In 1950 and 1960, "substandard" typically meant dilapidated units plus those units not dilapidated but lacking complete plumbing facilities.

Evaluation studies of the 1950 and 1960 censuses persuaded the bureau that the statistics on structural condition were unreliable and inaccurate, particularly in less populated areas. The bureau accordingly abandoned in the 1970 census any effort to rate the physical condition of homes. It did not, however, abandon its housing assessment activities for long. Beginning in 1973, the bureau has conducted an annual housing survey that includes both indicators of physical condition and measures of neighborhood quality. The Annual Housing Survey, conducted in conjunction with the Department of Housing and Urban Development, promises to provide better indicators of physical condition than those derived from earlier census measures. It samples about one of every thousand housing units in the United States, about sixty thousand in all, and collects far more details about the housing unit itself than in earlier census surveys. Moreover, since the same units are visited year after year, it is possible to trace over time improvements or deterioration in a given unit.

Some prewar experimental work conducted by the American Public Health Association has also led to a widely used method of housing assessment in the United States known as the American Public Health Association Appraisal Method. The Appraisal Method attempts to construct a cumulative penalty score on each structure and dwelling unit through the assignment of penalty points to conditions that fail to meet accepted housing standards. Specific point scores are determined by a panel of expert consultants. The method also permits separate evaluations of facilities, level of maintenance, and intensity of occupancy. In this approach certain deficiencies are defined as basic, and any dwelling that reveals deficiencies is classified "substandard." Several dozen American cities have used the A.P.H.A. Appraisal Method. The chief complaints about this method are that it is too expensive and time-consuming, and therefore unsuitable for widespread national use. It is more helpful in an intensive assessment of selective areas of poor housing than for city-wide application.

A related measure of housing quality and condition is found in the housing code and enforcement programs of the nation's cities. Housing codes set minimal standards of health and safety relating to the quality of basic facilities, level of maintenance, and occupancy of a housing unit. The most widely used code was first developed in 1952 by the American Public Health Association in cooperation with the U.S. Public Health Service. In 1954 fewer than one hundred cities had adopted housing codes. Provision of urban renewal funds in the Housing Act of 1954 required each applicant community to adopt building and housing codes and to formulate a plan for their enforcement. By 1968 about five thousand local governments had adopted housing codes.

Housing code standards are no more valid than those the Census Bureau has already abandoned: There are no generally agreed-upon definitions for such key terms as "adequate," "in safe condition," and "in good repair." The Douglas Commission, having studied the costs and effectiveness of code-enforcement programs, concluded that the

basic standards of a "decent home" were in need of refor-
mulation, and that a 25-year-old A.P.H.A. study is still considered the most thorough analytic work on the effects of
housing upon health. One concern about housing code standards is that they rest on judgments of public-health experts
that may better reflect cultural norms of the middle class
than either minimum health standards or the physical and
mental well-being of housing occupants.

As noted before, another way to talk about housing
standards and quality is in terms of the costs or price of
eliminating the defects in a substandard house. This approach has been taken by a number of economists, who try
to place a value on what consumers will pay for in a house.
We know, for example, that the market value or selling price
of a house is affected by its size, the number of rooms, lot
size, neighboring schools, nearness to employment and shopping, the quality of fire and police protection, and so forth.
To this list we can now add the quality and condition of the
house.

An early comprehensive effort to estimate the price of
housing quality was undertaken by Professors John F. Kain
and John M. Quigley. In a scorching St. Louis summer in
1967, they surveyed approximately 1,500 households and
dwelling units, collecting evidence covering thirty-nine
separate measures of physical or visual quality of housing
services, from which they constructed five aggregate
measures of differing aspects of housing quality. They concluded that property owners will pay from several hundred
up to as much as several thousand dollars more for a home
that is well above average quality for its type.

Other research supports these findings. A study of
homes sold in New Haven, Connecticut, between 1962 and
1969 found that houses that realtors rate as excellent, very
good, and good sell at premiums of $3,600, $3,000 and
$1,600, respectively, relative to houses rated fair or poor. A
study of single-family residences in Boston using local assess-

ment records also demonstrates a market premium for better than average quality homes, with a corresponding penalty for units of below average quality.

Pausing for a moment, let's weave together the disparate strands in this discussion of standards of housing condition and quality. Implicit in the concept of a decent house is some minimum standard of quality beneath which no American should have to live. However, efforts to measure structural quality and physical condition of housing have been disjointed. Indicators and standards have been constantly altered, modified, eliminated altogether, or replaced by new ones. One cannot therefore compare precisely chronological changes in the quality of the nation's housing.

Still, any use of the evolving indicators to measure quality and condition shows remarkable improvements in housing quality during the last thirty years. The proportion of substandard housing—defined as dilapidated or lacking plumbing—declined from 49 percent in 1940 to only 7 percent by 1970. By 1973, only 5 percent of the nation's homes and apartments lacked complete plumbing facilities compared with 7 percent in 1970. William C. Baer has flatly stated that "clearly, such improvement in the physical quality of the stock is so great that substituting other indicators and standards will not markedly affect the magnitude and direction of the trend."

John C. Weicher, formerly Deputy Assistant Secretary for Economic Affairs at the Department of Housing and Urban Development (HUD), wrote in August 1977 that America has almost met the goal of a decent home for all Americans as originally envisaged in 1949: The few physically inadequate units that remain diminish rapidly each year. Between 1973 and 1975, for example, the number of homes lacking complete plumbing facilities fell from 3.65 to 2.86 percent; the number with exposed electrical wiring fell from 3.97 to 1.84 percent. By 1980, according to conventional definitions and measures, substandard housing may be substantially diminished. (See Figure 5.1.)

Figure 5.1. **Characteristics of Housing Stock, Total U.S.**
(1950, 1960, 1970)

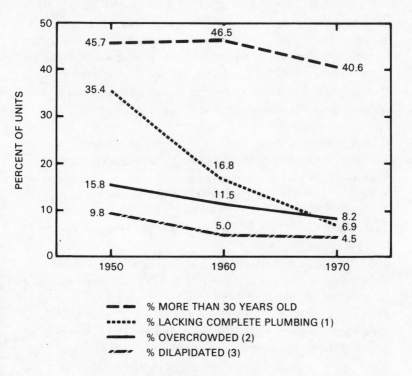

(1) LACKING COMPLETE PLUMBING — HOUSING UNITS WHICH LACK
ONE OR MORE PLUMBING FACILITIES OR HAVE A FACILITY USED
ALSO BY OCCUPANTS OF ANOTHER UNIT.

(2) OVERCROWDED — 1.01 OR MORE PERSONS PER ROOM.

(3) DILAPIDATED — HOUSING WHICH DOES NOT PROVIDE SAFE AND
ADEQUATE SHELTER, AND ENDANGERS HEALTH, SAFETY, OR
WELL BEING OF OCCUPANTS. DEFECTS ARE SO CRITICAL OR
WIDESPREAD THAT THE STRUCTURE SHOULD BE EXTENSIVELY
REPAIRED, REBUILT, OR TORN DOWN.

Source: Department of Commerce, Bureau of the Census, *Census of Housing,*
1950, 1960, 1970.

Raymond Struyk, a senior HUD official formerly with the Urban Institute in Washington, D.C., has explored housing conditions of older Americans. Using evidence collected in the 1973 Annual Housing Survey, he shows that the elderly are only modestly less well housed than the population at large, with the disproportionate share of structural defects concentrated in rural areas. Differences between elderly and younger households, both in terms of size and quality of housing, are not large—and in fact are much smaller than one would expect on the basis of their respective incomes. Altogether, about 17 percent of the city folks, and about 30 percent of those in the country, live in homes that need major repairs or that endure unpleasant neighborhood problems. And, as Weicher shows, these percentages diminish with each passing year.

The incidence of serious housing deficiencies of elderly homeowners, as revealed in the 1974 Annual Housing Survey, is minimal and parallels the elderly's own self-portrait in the previous chapter. Heating and plumbing equipment in their homes are somewhat inferior to that of younger homeowners, but they enjoy superior electrical facilities. Added up, the differences in the quality of their homes are insignificant.

Housing Deficiencies of Elderly-Owned Homes (*Based on 1974 Annual Housing Surveys*)

No bedroom privacy	0.2%
No complete plumbing facilities	0.4
No complete kitchen facilities	2.0
Interior ceiling and walls with open holes or cracks	3.0
Interior floors with holes	1.0
Roof water leakage	5.0
Exposed electrical wiring	4.0
Lack electric wall outlets in each room	6.0
No piped equipment breakdown	4.0

Taken at face value, the Annual Housing Survey gives little cause for public concern about the caliber of housing that our parents and grandparents long ago bought and today maintain. Still, standards of housing quality inevitably rise as the well-being of society improves. The stock of substandard housing can be summarily increased by simply upgrading the minimally acceptable notion of a decent home. Indeed, with the improvements of housing condition since 1940, the concept of decency has been broadened to incorporate heretofore disregarded neighborhood problems. However, even in the face of a more exacting standard of minimum housing condition, all American homeowners, and elderly homeowners in particular, are substantially better housed than ever before in our history. This pattern of improvement should persist for the foreseeable future.

A final note before moving on. Housing standards, as an analytic concept, embody a good deal of arbitrariness and subjective judgment that often reflect social, political, and economic values, as well as a society's wealth that might be allocated to housing. HUD officials readily acknowledge that no definite estimate can be given for the number of elderly whose homes fail to meet minimum standards set by society, because no one set of criteria rigidly determines "good" or "standard" quality housing. Analysts may count "key indicators" of housing deficiencies, but these must not be equated with the concept of a substandard or a decent home.

Overcrowding. Overcrowding is the second concept invoked to identify decent or substandard housing. Persons per room (PPR), an indicator of crowding, has remained in use throughout the century; the standard, however, has changed markedly with the passage of time. A home was considered to be overcrowded in the 1934 Real Property Inventories if the number of its occupants exceeded three persons per room. Densities exceeding two persons per room defined overcrowding in the 1940 and 1950 censuses, which fell to one and one-half in 1960 and 1970. There is pressure from several public and academic authorities to lower the standard to one person per room. Even in the face of more and more stringent standards of overcrowding, the American Public Health Association has not changed its limit of no more than two persons per room during the last forty years. There is dissension, not consensus, on the appropriate choice of a standard to signify overcrowding, which reflects variety in personal opinions and taste rather than true expertise in medicine and social planning.

Note that an overcrowded house is not synonymous with a dilapidated one. An overcrowded unit may or may not be physically sound; it simply shelters too many people. Moreover, simple changes can relieve overcrowding—the addition of a room, grown children moving out, a smaller family buying the same house. As single-person households increase in number, a decline in the incidence of over-crowding will correspondingly register. Against the standard of 1.50 persons per room, only 1 percent of all Americans live in overcrowded quarters in 1975. On the most extreme standard of 1.01 persons per room, overcrowding fell by half from 16 percent in 1950 to 8 percent of all families in 1970. Americans, of all the world's peoples, enjoy the most spacious accommodations.

Overcrowding as a signal of deficient housing rests on a premise of social hygiene which contends that cramming large numbers of persons into small quarters is mentally and physically unhealthy. Professor Eugene Meehan, explaining why the Pruitt-Igoe housing projects were such devastating failures in St. Louis, illustrates this contention. Meehan charges that crowding nine to ten persons in a poorly ventilated, 900-square-foot apartment encourages destructive tenant behavior. In Hong Kong, though, the density of public housing is four- to fivefold that of Pruitt-Igoe. At the rate of 24 square feet per adult in the older units, and only 35 square feet per adult in the newer units, a family of five may lie in one room consisting of 120 square feet in a hot and humid climate. But Hong Kong public-housing tenants are neither destructive nor ill and thus belie the overcrowding premise of unsuitable housing.

In any event, it makes no sense to talk of overcrowding among elderly homeowners, who, we have found, typically enjoy somewhere between five and seven rooms per household. Even by the most rigorous standard of 1.01 persons per room, one would be hard pressed to find more than a handful of overcrowded elderly homeowners in the United States. Ninety-one percent of all elderly homeowners enjoy two or more bedrooms in their house, along with a minimum of a kitchen, living room, and bathroom.

Ability to pay. A third dimension in the calculus of adequate housing is "ability to pay for housing." Its underlying premise is that housing expenditures must be kept within certain limits to prevent economic hardship to low-income families. If housing costs are too high, poor families will not have enough money in their household budget for food, medical treatment, clothing, transportation, and other necessities.

"Ability to pay" is measured by a formula that compares rent with income. A month's rent should not exceed a week's pay is the historical precursor to the present-day 25 percent ratio—or 35 percent for elderly and single-person households—of rent to income. As housing conditions have improved and overcrowding declined, ability to pay has come increasingly into vogue to signal that poor people are financially overburdened. Note that this concept applies only to renters, not to owners. We do not have comparable information or standards for the expenditure-to-income ratio for homeowners. Still, ability to pay enjoys widespread intellectual currency today because it is the only dimension of housing standards that shows a worsening state: Since 1949, the number and proportion of people who exceed the 25 percent rent-to-income ratio has increased. This may be less surprising when we consider that the number paying a higher proportion of their income for rent occurs precisely with improvements in physical quality; people are, in short, better housed. The shift in discussion from physical condition to financial burden is confirmation that the great majority of homes now meet all acceptable levels of quality; current policy emphasizes the reduction of housing costs for low-income families.

Neighborhood quality. Historical interest in physical condition and overcrowding is giving way to a broader concern for overall neighborhood quality. In view of the fact that traditional standards are met in the majority of homes, any new large-scale government involvement with housing requires a different standard with which to legitimize its conduct. Neighborhood quality affords that new criterion. Its application to urban life can be used to show greater housing needs than otherwise now exist. Families who live in physically adequate housing may be said to live in a "bad" neighborhood, whose ills can only be remedied with appropriate public intervention. Since 1973 the Annual Housing Surveys have collected this information and report that neighborhood deficiencies are ten to fifteen times as great as deficiencies in individual housing structures. Specific undesirable conditions tabulated in the Annual Housing Survey include noise, heavy traffic, odors, litter, abandoned buildings, deteriorating housing, commercial or industrial activity, streets in disrepair, inadequate street lighting, and crime. This new emphasis on neighborhood quality is evident in the 1974 Housing and Community Development Act, which authorizes block grants to communities for comprehensive urban programs that include both housing programs and supporting neighborhood facilities.

If standards of housing condition and quality vary widely, reflecting different cultural, political, and economic perspectives in any society, techniques relating to what are good and bad environments are subject to even wider differences of opinion. Assessing the social characteristics of neighborhoods may become more important in future evaluations of housing, but any environmental index is likely to evince a good deal of arbitrariness. Moreover, residents are likely to see neighborhood quality in their community in quite different terms from professional people who compile and conduct studies, especially in neighborhoods where outsiders may have little acquaintance with the residents' priorities.

Nor do we yet have an accepted theory of neighborhood decline. Leading analysts disagree on the major causes of poor housing. Professor Richard F. Muth of Stanford University suggests that one cause is the conversion of high-quality residences to multi-family smaller units to accommodate an increase in demand for housing by low-income families who have moved into the central cities, a transition made possible and profitable by the movement of high-income persons to the suburbs. Another cause of poor-quality housing is that landlords may defer maintenance and repair and thus allow buildings to deteriorate. Muth rejects the arguments that age and obsolescence of the dwelling unit, along with the presence of undesirable neighborhood features, cause poor-quality housing.

The contrary view that relates age and obsolescence of housing to neighborhood decline has been set forth by Professors James W. Hughes and Kenneth D. Bleakly, Jr. They pinpoint age of housing as one direct cause of neighborhood decline. Other forces include rising home maintenance costs, owners seeking more fashionable residential options, and a decline in neighborhood morale, which culminate in owner disinvestment. The outcome in a number of large metropolitan areas is a massive supply of outmoded, obsolescent housing built around the turn of the century for different social groups who no longer inhabit these structures.

Several external forces also contribute to neighborhood

decline. These include in-migrations of different populations—lower-status groups move in as the most mobile move out—and commercial land use that invades adjacent residential neighborhoods. As neighborhoods age physically and socially, efforts to improve them decline. Structural defects increase, older housing is adapted to higher-density usage, poorer households increasingly move in, and racial/ethnic change accelerates. Decay sets in and ultimately may lead to abandonment.

Given that we have no single, well-accepted explanation of neighborhood decline, it is not surprising that urban renewal, model cities, community block grants, or a host of other public and private community efforts have failed to halt urban decay. Standards of good and bad features in any environment are hard to come by, which makes almost any measure of neighborhood quality highly subjective and arbitrary.

A Professional Rating of Elderly-Owned Homes

We have stressed that there is no such thing as any objective correct definition of housing quality among the 1,575 elderly homeowners we talked with. One owner's definition of adequate housing may be too stringent, or too lenient, for another. Still, despite the historically changing standards of decent housing, it is nonetheless worthwhile to try to distill a more explicit definition of good housing and develop a rating technique to assess housing deficiencies in a reliable manner, if we are to talk of housing quality in any objective sense. Housing goals and programs rest upon these standards, however dynamic, so it will be useful to compare the best professional evaluation we can conduct with that put forth by the homeowner himself.

Reliability. To measure the "objective" need for repairs and maintenance, we obtained and substantially revised the rating scale instrument prepared for the Experimental Housing Allowance Program, the most comprehensive instrument then in use. To insure that our field staff correctly understood how to apply the instrument, extensive training sessions were held and a detailed surveyor manual prepared. In addition, a 10 percent re-evaluation of the sample was carried out at each site by one or more professional housing specialists.

We compared each of these follow-up inspections with the Housing Evaluation Form (or HEF, for short) completed for the home on an item-by-item basis. In the aggregate we achieved over 90 percent reliability in all but a handful of items. In the entire survey, only one evaluator (in San Francisco) was judged significantly less reliable than we found overall, and for this reason we removed his evaluations from the sample. The extremely high levels of reliability give us confidence that we may accept the "objective" ratings as just that—reliable estimates of what professional housing specialists would obtain with the Housing Evaluation Form.

Recall that each elderly homeowner gave a general assessment of housing adequacy or named a specific item he felt needed repair or maintenance work. The Housing Evaluations supplied vastly greater detail on the condition of the different features of each house, permitting both overall ratings of the major systems—plumbing, electrical, heating, roof and gutters, basic structure, exterior, kitchen, garage and driveway—and specific ratings of each of the individual housing items that enter into a major system, for example, electric fixtures, light switches, fusebox, etc. We structured the homeowner questionnaires and the HEF rating scales to permit direct comparisons on both general housing systems and specific household items.

The measures. A review of Census Bureau publications and numerous scholarly studies of housing suggest three sets of categories from which we might try to distill an objective statement of the condition of a house. The first set is made up of "basic facilities," which consists of such housing components as complete kitchen facilities, a complete private bathroom, hot water, central heating (except in warmer climate regions), at least one bedroom, and one other room, typically a living room or sitting room. The notion of "basic facilities" is predicated upon the recognition that an adequate house in contemporary America should have a minimum core of features. Absence of one or more of these items means that the house is inadequate—it does not meet the objectively specified minimum standards of a decent home. Figure 5.2 sets forth the rating scale items that are combined to produce an overall measure of "basic facilities."

A second set of evaluations bears upon hazardous and dangerous features in a house that directly threaten the safety of its occupants or render the house unlivable—for instance, a collapsing wall. Exposed wires, faulty handrails,

FIGURE 5.2.   **Elements of "Basic Facilities"**

Plumbing:	a working toilet
	a working shower with hot water
	a working wash basin with hot water
	a working kitchen sink with hot water
	a working water heater
Electric:	working electric outlets in living room, bathroom, kitchen, dining room, and bedroom
Heating:	a working source of heat
	minimum adequate temperature maintenance in home
Roof & gutter:	——
Basic structure:	——
Exterior:	——
Kitchen:	a working stove
	a working refrigerator
	a working sink with hot water
Garage & driveway:	——

leaking gas pipes, and other defects pose a personal risk to the elderly resident. Figure 5.3 enumerates the elements that enter into the determination of a "health or safety hazard."

A third and final category of household ratings concerns those housing deficiencies that need correction but which pose neither an immediate major safety or health hazard to the individual nor a critical risk to his remaining in the home. Corroded plumbing fixtures, a leaking roof, cracked plaster, and peeling paint illustrate this third set of needed repairs. (See Figure 5.4)

Housing experts may argue about the distinctions among the three categories, but we think it important and extremely relevant to distinguish between defects that are immediately serious and those that are not. To review, three definitions of objectively rated housing conditions are de-

FIGURE 5.3. **Elements of "Health or Safety Hazard"**

Plumbing:	——
Electric:	presence of defective electrical outlets
	presence of defective electrical switches
	presence of defective electrical fixtures
Heating:	inoperative thermostat
	a major defect in heating source
Roof & gutter:	roof surface in major disrepair
	roof structure in major disrepair
	chimney and flue in major disrepair
Basic structure:	floor surface in major disrepair
	floor structure in major disrepair
	stairs in major disrepair
	foundation in major disrepair
	inadequate stair lighting
Exterior:	exterior wall structure in major disrepair
	entranceway in major disrepair
	exterior stairs in major disrepair
	porch needs replacement
	window(s) need replacement
Kitchen:	——
Garage & driveway:	garage in major disrepair

FIGURE 5.4.   **Elements of "Long-Term Repair Needs"**

Plumbing:	a broken toilet a broken shower a broken wash basin lack of adequate waterproofing in bathroom a broken hot-water heater
Electric:	——
Heating:	heating outlet in disrepair no thermostat present
Roof & gutter:	——
Basic structure:	ceiling surface in major disrepair ceiling structure in major disrepair wall surface in major disrepair wall structure in major disrepair inadequate hall lighting
Exterior:	exterior paint needs replacement exterior wall surface in major disrepair porch in disrepair storm windows need replacement has no working storm windows (only for Dayton, Pittsfield, Philadelphia, and New Ulm)
Kitchen:	stove in major disrepair refrigerator in major disrepair sink in major disrepair
Garage & driveway:	driveway in major disrepair

rived from the completed Housing Evaluation Forms: "basic facilities," "hazardous or dangerous features," and "housing systems requiring major repairs, but not posing short-term threat to staying in one's own home."

Results.   Table 5.1 lists the percentage of homes in each site that lacks basic plumbing, electrical, heating, and kitchen facilities. A defect in any portion of one of the separate dimensions means that the entire system is given a defective rating. For example, the absence of a working light switch in the bathroom exemplifies the absence of a mini-

TABLE 5.1. Percentages of Houses Lacking Basic Facilities

HOUSING SYSTEMS	PHILA-DELPHIA	SAN FRANCISCO	DAYTON	TULSA	PITTS-FIELD	NEW ULM	ORANGE-BURG	ALL SITES
Plumbing	7	8	18	11	11	13	50	18
Electrical	6	3	13	2	2	13	57	14
Heating	8	7	12	9	4	5	76	18
Roof & gutter	—	—	—	—	—	—	—	—
Basic structure	—	—	—	—	—	—	—	—
Exterior	—	—	—	—	—	—	—	—
Kitchen	3	8	13	10	3	8	47	14
Garage & driveway	—	—	—	—	—	—	—	—
Total (with any problem)	17	18	34	18	14	20	93	32

105

mally essential component in the electrical system of a house. One or more omissions for each facility means a defective rating for the entire system. The totals presented in the bottom line of the table are obtained by adding every housing unit that appears in any of the four systems at least once; no house, however, is counted twice. Thus, in Philadelphia, 17 percent of all houses have at least one (and sometimes more than one) housing system that lacks an element of a basic facility. Overall, the figure is 32 percent. Homes in Pittsfield are best-off, homes in Orangeburg correspondingly worst-off.

The second definition of objectively rated condition of housing units addresses potential safety hazards or dangers to the occupants. As the bottom line in Table 5.2 points out, typically about one house in three has at least one potential hazard to safety. The great bulk of the hazards lie, in descending order, in the basic structure, the exterior, the roof and gutter, and the electrical system. Again, homes in Orangeburg typify less satisfactory rural housing.

The third definition of objective housing condition is the need for major repairs to one or more of the integral elements in the respective housing systems. This third definition is distinguished from the first in that it refers to the presence of a problem—for example, a defective toilet—rather than to the absence of a feature, and from the second definition in that the defect poses no immediate health or safety hazard. In the long term, left untended, these problems may accelerate the deterioration of a house. Table 5.3 shows what proportion of homes require major repairs to forestall long-term deterioration.

A summary of all objective measures, including several combinations of categories, appears in Table 5.4. Note throughout the much higher incidence of defects in Orangeburg County compared with city housing.

Why do the Housing Evaluation Forms uncover a much higher incidence of unsatisfactory conditions than the elderly

TABLE 5.2. Percentages of Houses with Safety Hazards

HOUSING SYSTEMS	PHILA-DELPHIA	SAN FRANCISCO	DAYTON	TULSA	PITTS-FIELD	NEW ULM	ORANGE-BURG	ALL SITES
Plumbing	—	—	—	—	—	—	—	—
Electrical	9	8	16	5	2	2	18	9
Heating	3	1	3	3	1	1	12	4
Roof & gutter	9	6	13	16	13	12	34	15
Basic structure	20	14	24	8	14	21	62	24
Exterior	8	11	12	20	10	4	48	17
Kitchen	—	—	—	—	—	—	—	—
Garage & driveway	2	2	5	4	6	1	3	3
Total (with any problem)	33	30	43	32	28	32	75	40

TABLE 5.3. Percentages of Houses Potentially Requiring Major Long-Term Repairs

HOUSING SYSTEMS	PHILA-DELPHIA	SAN FRANCISCO	DAYTON	TULSA	PITTS-FIELD	NEW ULM	ORANGE-BURG	ALL SITES
Plumbing	5	5	12	10	1	4	22	9
Electrical	—	—	—	—	—	—	—	—
Heating	7	23	8	4	3	14	4	8
Roof & gutter	—	—	—	—	—	—	—	—
Basic structure	22	17	23	15	9	8	65	23
Exterior	20	23	35	16	23	17	58	28
Kitchen	3	8	13	10	3	3	33	10
Garage & driveway	2	4	3	5	1	0	6	3
Total (with any problem)	36	49	52	31	31	30	81	44

TABLE 5.4. Summary of Objective Ratings (Percentages)

	PHILA-DELPHIA	SAN FRANCISCO	DAYTON	TULSA	PITTS-FIELD	NEW ULM	ORANGE-BURG	ALL SITES
Lacking basic facilities	17	18	34	18	14	20	93	32
Safety hazards	35	30	43	32	28	32	75	40
Lacking basic facilities or having safety hazards	43	36	55	36	34	40	97	50
Requires major long-term repair	36	49	52	31	31	30	81	44
Any system defect	54	60	70	44	48	51	99	60

attribute to their own homes? One reason has to do with the definition of an objective housing defect: If any part of a housing system is lacking or defective, that entire system is rated inadequate. For example, the absence of a wash basin with hot water renders the entire plumbing system deficient, even though raters found the house could have a working toilet, a working shower with hot water, a working kitchen sink with hot water, and a working water heater. An elderly homeowner who has lived his entire life without a working wash basin might not regard his plumbing facilities as inadequate for that reason. Figures 5.2, 5.3, and 5.4 break down each housing dimension into its several components; one defect scores the entire system faulty.

Another reason why the HEFs yield higher scores is that professional standards are invariably more demanding than those of the general population. The rating scale rests on professional criteria of housing condition. Decision and policy makers inside and outside of government, being themselves from the better-off sectors of society, not only demand high standards of provision of public and private services to meet what they consider their own essential needs, but also find it difficult to think of provision for the rest of the population in terms of standards that are not equally high. Thus, application of any professionally developed rating scale would yield a higher incidence of housing deficiencies than that obtained by polling all but perhaps the wealthiest of homeowners.

Nonetheless, the HEF ratings are a reliable, professionally derived statement of housing quality. Specific measures of adequacy can be made more, or less, stringent; still, the overall ratings reveal whose homes are in above-average or below-average condition. If we wanted to mount a national housing repair program, the HEF scores would direct us to those whose homes are in worst condition, though they would not reveal whether or not the owners of those homes agree.

Why Are Homes Poorly Maintained?

In this section, we address the question of why some homes are well maintained and others are not. Before we assemble a composite picture relating housing quality to the characteristics of the homeowner, his house, and the kind of community in which he lives, we must first choose the appropriate measure of disrepair in which to couch this investigation: basic facilities, hazards, long-term repair problems, or some combination of the three.

In selecting a measure of condition, we want to avoid the imputation that homes are in excessively good or excessively bad shape, but recognize that any standard must be arbitrary. A measure of disrepair that combines all three categories would reveal the largest incidence of housing inadequacy; to use but one would reveal the least degree. We have chosen the union of the first two measures: We regard any home that lacks a required facility or presents a safety hazard as deficient in condition or quality, and hereafter use the term *critical defect* to reflect this joint measure. Although long-term repair needs, left uncorrected, ultimately become pressing, people readily adjust to peeling paint or chipped plaster. A direct threat to health or safety is postponed or disregarded only at personal risk, and the absence of a core facility makes a home inadequate by definition. Table 5.4 shows, overall, that half of all sampled homes have at least one critical defect. In Orangeburg County, this situation is near universal; in the urban areas and small towns only about one home in three has a problem of this kind. On the average, a home in our sample has slightly more than one system with a critical defect.

Recall the sole purpose of the Housing Evaluation Form: It provides an objective (on criteria of reliability) description of the house. The absence of a specific subset of problems

111

that make up "critical defects" is, in effect, a minimum standard of core facilities and safe habitation. Now we want to know who are the people that live in these homes, and how they differ from other older Americans whose homes are not well kept and safe.

It would be ideal to begin our analysis of housing condition by delineating a broadly accepted and statistically supported theory of housing decline. Unfortunately, no such theory exists. Indeed, as Professor Richard Muth has pointed out, "surprisingly little attention has been given to the causes of poor-quality housing." While we do not here formulate a theory of housing condition, we do seek to characterize statistically the various factors that are associated with poor housing.

Income. Some analysts have focused on income (or, more precisely, low-income) as a partial explanation of poor quality housing. First, low-income families have fewer dollars to spend on maintenance. But, second, a neighborhood of largely low-income families may be a cause of lower housing values and thus make it economically unwise for any one resident to invest to upkeep.

Figure 5.5 shows that the poorest families have four to five times as many problems as the richest. We can also put this relationship in a different way: 74 percent of all those in the lowest income bracket have homes with at least one critical defect, compared with only 27 to 34 percent for those in the two highest income brackets. This disparity between rich and poor holds true for each element in the house, whether it is the plumbing, heating, or electrical system.

Wealth. As Chapter 3 indicates, current income is only a partial measure of an older person's economic well-being. By spending their savings or other assets, homeowners are better able to pay the costs of home maintenance. It is not surprising, then, that wealthier homeowners live in better

Figure 5.5. Current Income and Critical Defects

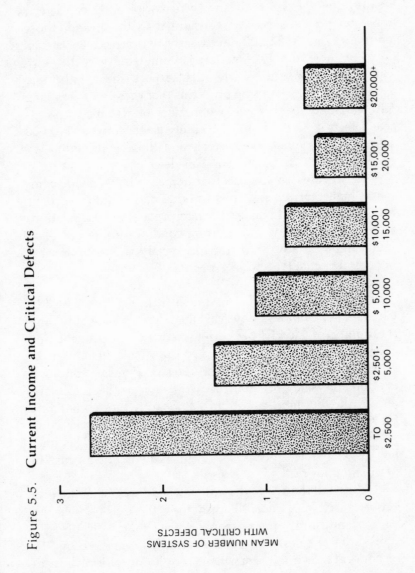

3

2

1

0

MEAN NUMBER OF SYSTEMS
WITH CRITICAL DEFECTS

TO
$2,500

$2,501-
5,000

$5,001-
10,000

$10,001-
15,000

$15,001-
20,000

$20,000+

kept homes. Those whose assets exceed $50,000 (excluding equity) average less than one system with a critical defect; those with no assets average more than three; and, those with assets up to $2,500 have nearly two defective systems.

For most elderly Americans, home equity is the principal form of wealth. As we might expect, those with more equity have fewer housing problems. For those with less than $10,000 in equity, the average number of systems with critical defects is 2.61. Those with equity assets between $10,000 and $20,000 average one defect, and those with equity exceeding $20,000 have but one-half defect.

Other research suggests that homes in better shape command higher prices and thus provide more equity for their owners. This finding makes the interpretation of the relationship between equity and housing condition more complex, requiring more advanced statistical analysis, which appears later in this chapter and in Appendix C.

Health and age. Let us move from wealth to health. Changes in health and physical capabilities presumably limit the ability of elderly persons to remain independent and properly maintain their homes. Looking at age directly, however, yields an especially delightful result: Housing condition is about the same for homeowners between the ages of 60 and 84. Ill-kept homes crop up significantly more often only for the over-85 population, and this small minority comprises less than 10 percent of all older Americans. This finding suggests that a person's age, in itself, is not a cause of declining housing.

Although the age of the homeowner does not distinguish between well-kept and ill-kept homes, those in poor health have significantly more troublesome homes. Figure 5.6 shows that persons in poor health—as signified by the respondent's own self-assessment, not by an objective medical exam—have homes with three times as many systems with critical defects as those in good to excellent health.

Figure 5.6. Health and Critical Defects

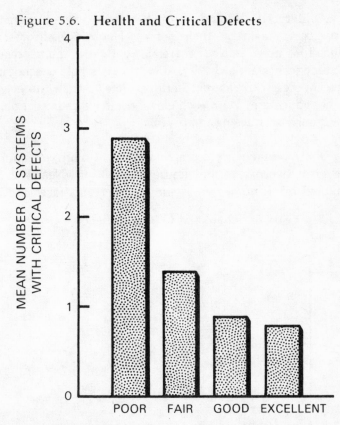

These results imply that self-perception of ill health may impede satisfactory maintenance. Increasing limitations of physical agility, strength, and ease of movement seemingly cramp an elderly person's ability or willingness to take care of his home.

Education. Factors apart from age, health, and financial status typically influence peoples' habits of consumption and choice of standards; among these, education may be the most important. While we have no reason to believe that schooling directly affects the housing choices of the elderly, it seems plausible to suppose that the more highly educated

115

have different tastes and, through higher incomes, a greater capacity to maintain their homes. Figure 5.7 shows that education does indeed correlate with the homeowner's maintenance standards. Those with little to no schooling have homes with far more critical defects than those with higher education. With each elevation in years in schooling, the quality of housing improves.

Race. Singularly dramatic in this entire investigation is the tie between race and housing condition. Nearly every sampled black homeowner (some 95 percent) faces at least

Figure 5.7. **Years of School and Critical Defects**

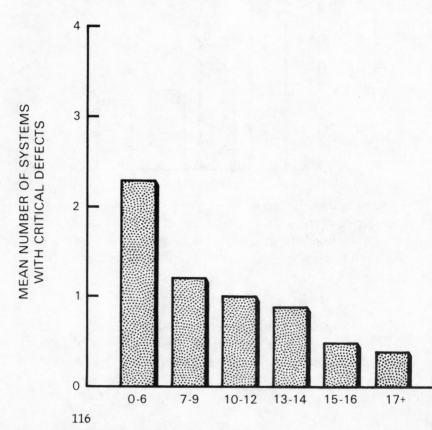

one critical defect in his home, as against only 44 percent among whites. Figure 5.8 shows that the number of systems with critical defects in black-owned homes is four times that in white-owned homes.

House and community. We have looked at some characteristics of old people to see which ones correlate with standards of upkeep; we now move on to some characteristics of the house and community. Recall that about 88 percent of all elderly-owned homes were built before 1960. In our sample the average age of a house is slightly more than 45 years.

Figure 5.8. **Race and Critical Defects**

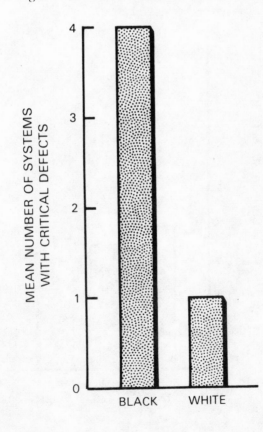

117

As individuals develop gerontologically related disorders, so too do homes show symptoms of aging. Most prospective purchasers of older homes anticipate more routine maintenance than if they were to purchase a newer home. Older homes are frequently devoid of complete kitchen and bathroom facilities and often have out-of-date electrical and plumbing installations.

Housing experts have argued that age and obsolescence are causes of declining housing quality. Figure 5.9 offers some supporting evidence. Homes that have reached their sixty-fifth birthday have nearly one and one-half times as

Figure 5.9. Year House Built and Critical Defects

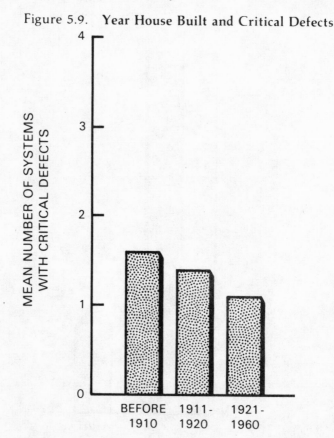

many critical system defects as do those in the youngest group.

The nature of the community in which a house is located may affect its condition by influencing the maintenance decisions made by the homeowner. Several scholars have suggested that neighborhood housing decline reflects (and is reflected in) changes in the makeup of the local population. The major focus of their research has been on the impact of declining community income. However, some have also suggested that in urban areas the influx of blacks is a harbinger of decreasing income and predicts housing decline.

Our data support both contentions. An examination of the incomes of neighborhood residents (in the five SMSAs we sampled, for which the figures are available) disclosed that low income and poor housing quality are linked together. Homes located in census tracts with median incomes below $10,000 average 1.2 systems with critical defects; those in tracts with median incomes between $10,000 and $15,000 average 0.7; and, those over $15,000 average 0.3 defects. The same pattern holds for neighborhood racial composition. The average number of defects in tracts with fewer than 25 percent black residents is 0.7. The figure rises to one defect in those tracts containing between one-quarter and three-quarters black residents and jumps to 2.4 defects in tracts with more than three-quarters black residents.

Census tract information is not available in New Ulm and Orangeburg. We therefore asked our respondents to describe the racial composition of their neighborhood on a five point scale ranging between "all white" and "all nonwhite." The same results appear. Homeowners who live in self-described "all white" areas average less than one system with a critical defect. With each successive category of more "nonwhite," the mean number of defects increases. Homes in "all nonwhite" areas average more than three and one-half defects.

Our analysis thus far reveals that such factors as education, financial status, and health correlate with poor housing condition. It is, however, somewhat more complex to estimate accurately the contribution of each of these factors when they are considered simultaneously. For example, limited assets, little education, and low incomes are not only correlated with the presence of housing defects, they are also correlated with each other. It is thus necessary to disentangle the independent impact of these separate factors by going beyond the analyses thus far presented.

We have noted the apparently different housing standards in the several sites and thus want to separate the effect of these differing community standards from the influence of homeowner and house characteristics on housing condition. Another difficulty is the reciprocal tie between home equity and housing condition: Homeowners with more equity are better able to maintain their homes, and better maintained homes command higher prices (producing greater equity). Finally, we should note that such neighborhood characteristics as the presence of low income or minority group families may not directly affect housing condition, but indirectly may influence the decisions about home maintenance of elderly homeowners.

We can resolve these issues with a system of simultaneous equations that includes the variables we have considered and others. We present the details of this analysis in Appendix C and summarize the major results below.

Most, but not all, of the foregoing relationships remain important. As before, the age of the owner has no systematic effect on housing condition. However, owners who say they are in poor health have more housing defects. We believe that an elderly person's subjective assessment of health influences his or her capacity for home maintenance. Education, in the refined analysis, does not have an independent effect on housing condition. We believe that economic status and choice of neighborhood are the mechanisms by which better educated persons consume higher quality housing.

Race remains a key variable. When all other factors are taken into account (including financial status), blacks live in homes that have on average at least one more critical defect than do whites.

What is the explanation for the substantially less satisfactory condition of black-owned homes? Since differences in economic status, education, health, age of home, and community have all been considered in this analysis, we must look elsewhere for the answer.

Several possibilities come to mind. It may be that the historical practice of discrimination against blacks in the single-family-residence housing markets is being reflected in our measure of housing condition. In the past, black buyers may have had fewer homes to choose from, and other studies suggest that they bought less housing for the same dollar. Perhaps black owners never found it financially worthwhile to improve their homes to the same standard as whites because of the effects of discrimination on housing values and the inability to recover this additional investment on resale.

It is also conceivable that blacks have suffered and perhaps still suffer restrictions and discrimination in their ability to buy repair and maintenance services. In rural South Carolina, for example, only a handful of firms engage in home maintenance work. Unfortunately, we have no evidence one way or the other that these firms discriminate against black customers. Recall that the elderly themselves, in Orangeburg County and elsewhere, were satisfied with both the availability and the quality of their community repair services.

A third explanation may reflect differences in taste or preference. Black elderly homeowners may choose to spend more of their income than whites on other goods and services and therefore have less to spend for housing. Or black home-owners may simply reflect a tradition in which home upkeep is not a high priority.

The full explanation probably includes some of these and other reasons. The facts, however, are beyond dispute: Black-owned housing is in much worse condition than that owned by whites, even after taking into account the economic status, health, and education of the homeowner, the community in which he lives, and the age of the house.

The total economic status of the homeowner, including current income and both forms of wealth, *does* affect housing condition. However, an interesting pattern of impact emerges among the three measures we considered. We find that the statistical effect of income does not significantly differ from that of equity in the home or of other assets. But the effect of assets in the form of equity is greater than that of wealth in its other forms. That is, homeowners are more likely to translate wealth in their homes into better quality homes than they are to use other assets to improve them.

Moving from homeowner to house characteristics, we find that older homes have more problems, although the magnitude of this impact is small. We estimate that a home acquires approximately one more system with a critical defect for every hundred years it ages.

Finally, we note the major differences among the survey sites. It remains true that homes in Orangeburg County are in worse condition, even after considering both the characteristics of the homeowner and the house itself. Again, the different housing standards of the rural site are clearly reflected in our statistical results.

A Note on Economic Status and Housing Condition

Chapter 3 included an analysis of the economic well-being of the elderly homeowners we sampled. In this chapter we have found that owners with fewer financial resources live in lower quality housing. Now we want to estimate the proportion of elderly homeowners that are both poor and live in poor housing.

Recall that when assets are considered, only 11 percent of our respondents have potential incomes below the official poverty line. The great majority of these persons have homes with critical defects. Extending the approach set forth in Chapter 3 (which takes account of missing data on homeowner wealth), we conclude that about 10 percent of our respondents are poor and have homes with critical defects.

Recall that nearly half of all homes have a serious problem. This means most homes with critical defects are owned by elderly Americans who, by our definition, are not poor. To some, this may seem anomalous, but we are not overly troubled. In the next chapter we explore one reason why many nonpoor homeowners live in homes of lower quality. In Part Three we discuss what to do about it.

6

Lay versus Expert

Do OLD PEOPLE LIVE in decent housing? When we talk with the elderly, the answer is largely yes, excepting maybe those who live in the countryside and those who are not white. When we talk with housing professionals, a different story unfolds: Perhaps as many as one-half of all elderly-owned homes are seriously defective either in their facilities or condition of repair. In terms of this second view, many of the elderly are indecently housed. Which of these two views is correct? Which one defines the "true" extent of the problem?

Not too long ago, each person took care of his own housing needs without any assistance from the government. Since 1949, however, "a decent home for every American family" has become the hallmark of national housing policy, and the government has become an active partner with the housing industry in an effort to further this goal. But if we do not know how to identify inadequate or indecent housing, then we do not know whom to help, how many people need help, or the cost of improving substandard housing. The goal of decent housing for all must remain elusive.

What is so important about the opinions of the elderly? Until recently, planners typically paid little attention to the views of those who are most affected by their decisions. The government does not attack such social problems as alcoholism, drug addiction, falling educational standards, poor health, or substandard housing by asking for the opinions of drunks, drug addicts, dropouts, the sick, and so forth. It relies on professional expertise to define ˙the problem, measure its extent, and propose practical solutions.

Many man-years of work and hundreds of millions of dollars of spending have not eliminated alcoholism, drug addiction, school dropouts, or a host of other social ills. Expertise and specialization is not enough. We have found in our own research and increasingly in the work of others a recognition that many of the poor, the sick, the elderly, the publicly housed, to name a few, do not want those services and programs that government officials, policy analysts, professional service givers, and university professors think they should have. Medicine must be swallowed to cure. Books must be read to inform. People who do not sign up for government programs or are unwilling participants generally do not benefit from them. And many do not participate because they do not want—in their own terms, do not need—government benefits or simply don't want to get involved with the government.

This book represents a rare opportunity to compare two distinct evaluations of housing—one reflecting professional standards, the other the opinions of the elderly. The degree to which the two perspectives differ or converge will determine, in large measure, if it makes sense for the government to intervene in the housing affairs of older Americans and in what way.

The Needs/Preferences Mismatch

How can we best describe how close to or far apart from each other are the opinions of the elderly about their homes and a professional assessment of the same homes? To talk about these similarities and differences we will use the expression "need/preferences mismatch." Recall the derivation of these terms. *Preferences* represent the tastes, values, or opinions individuals have—in this case the standard of housing they want to maintain. Moreover, these preferences are

125

constrained by an individual's financial resources, which dictate that he choose among competing alternatives on which to spend his money. *Needs*, on the other hand, are the judgments of experts that establish minimum standards—in this case the search for standards of decent housing. But needs, unlike preferences, are based on abstract criteria that are not encumbered by considerations of cost. Thus, *needs* will serve as shorthand for objective problems (that is, a professional house rating), and *preferences* will signify the opinions of the elderly themselves. A needs/preferences mismatch on housing condition thus counts the proportion of objectively rated defects that the elderly see as perfectly adequate.

Figure 6.1 illustrates the needs/preferences mismatch in its entirety for the seven major housing systems. Look at the first column on the left-hand side of the figure, which shows the needs/preferences mismatch for plumbing facilities. The total height of the column shows the percentage of homes that have a "critical defect" in the plumbing system; in this example, the raters found that 16 percent of all homes had one or more objective plumbing defects. In the language of needs, 16 percent of all homes *need* work to fix some plumbing fault. Look next at the crosshatched segment of the column. It signifies how many older persons say the plumbing system in their house is inadequate—about 3 percent in this case. Thus the elderly's own *preferences* about plumbing show a much smaller requirement for plumbing repairs.

The unshaded portion of the column is that proportion of respondents who do not concur that an objective need for repair of any given housing characteristic exists. For example, 81 percent of all elderly who live in homes that need a plumbing repair do not, in their own terms, reveal a preference for plumbing repairs. A housing expert might say that 81 percent of the elderly homeowners do not have the necessary knowledge to be able to recognize a serious problem in their home; or that older people have standards of

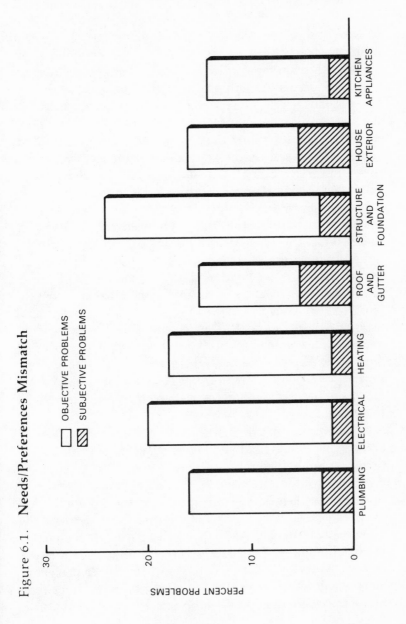

Figure 6.1. Needs/Preferences Mismatch

PERCENT PROBLEMS

OBJECTIVE PROBLEMS
SUBJECTIVE PROBLEMS

PLUMBING
ELECTRICAL
HEATING
ROOF AND GUTTER
STRUCTURE AND FOUNDATION
HOUSE EXTERIOR
KITCHEN APPLIANCES

housing condition that are lower than those considered minimally acceptable by society; or that they are too old to care and thus don't want to admit to the presence of a real problem; or that they are spending their money foolishly on the wrong things and neglecting their homes.

Look across the entire row of columns. The mismatch (the unshaded area) is very large for every part of the house: It ranges from a low of 64 percent for roof and gutter to as high as 87 percent for electrical items. Application of housing standards that rest on the preferences of the elderly yields a much lower incidence of inadequate housing than a corresponding application of a professional, middle-class standard. The latter finds anywhere from two to ten times as many housing problems as that acknowledged by the elderly themselves. We should note that this pattern of the needs/preferences mismatch emerges regardless of the specific measures we have used.

Where are the areas of mismatch the most and least extensive? Such housing aspects as roof and gutters and general exterior features show the least extent of disagreement; conversely, interior features provide the greatest incidence of mismatch. As a passing note, the mismatch is less prominent in rural Orangeburg County; not only do homes there *need* more work, rural southern elderly see more inadequacies in those homes.

In some settings, it is possible to imagine that an elderly homeowner would hold to a higher standard of maintenance than that established by society as a bottom-line measure of acceptable condition. How many elderly homeowners find some part of their home inadequate even though application of an objective rating scale finds no need for repairs? The answer is very few. To all intents and purposes, there is no mismatch about the satisfactory aspects of a home between owner and analyst. Excepting roof and gutters, 95 percent or more of all elderly respondents regard those parts of their house that were rated to be in objectively good condition as subjectively adequate. To repeat, if the rater says that the house does not need repairs, then the owner says the house is adequate. These results are to be expected since the subjective standards of the homeowners are, in practice, lower than those contained in the definition of "critical defects." Only in New Ulm, and just for exterior features at that, do homeowners adopt personal standards that are higher than those derived from professional considerations. These small-town, north-central U.S. residents regard slight peeling of paint as unacceptable.

When the needs/preferences mismatch is performed on a more detailed level for the twenty-eight separate elements each owner was asked about, the exact same pattern of results was obtained. With few exceptions, three-quarters or more of all respondents—urban and rural, large city or small town, east, west, north, or south—disagree with ratings that point to a need for repair. Housing Evaluations Forms may demonstrate that stoves, refrigerators, light switches, thermostats, floors, walls, ceilings, stairs, and so forth need repair, but in three-fourths of these instances, the owners say that no repairs are required.

In any argument, different assumptions imply different conclusions. In this survey of elderly homeowners, two separate standards of housing quality—one showing a *need* and one revealing a *preference*—permit two radically distinct appraisals about the condition of their homes.

Additional Evidence

The needs/preferences mismatch characterizes not only a clash in perspectives about housing standards but also about the full range of housing and other services that local, state, and national governments provide. Its central thesis is that experts and social planners often impute to all people, especially the poor, the elderly, and minorities, a minimum level of consumption of certain goods and services—what must be their basic human needs—even if these groups of people reject these items as necessary or desirable. The related concept of "helping" the poor, the elderly, or minorities, of providing more services and opportunities for them, implies that their present consumption falls short of some socially desirable level, that of middle-class America. In this vein, gerontological and other social research has often sought to determine the needs of the elderly. As expected, specific recommendations of assistance are couched in language that appeals to administrators or social workers. One rarely encounters the view that the aged, the poor, or minorities have a life style that is actually preferred to that of other segments of society.

Other studies show that needs professionally imputed to the elderly and the poor do not necessarily correspond with their stated preferences. In a survey of elderly inner-city residents of Rochester, New York, the vast majority of the elderly poor did not consider themselves to need substantial services and assistance, despite the claims of several dozen agencies within the city. In the presumed problem areas of transportation, feeding themselves, getting adequate medical care, social isolation, and housing satisfaction, over 80 percent reported no difficulty.

Another study completed in the early 1970s compared perceptions of the priorities of service needs of a sample of urban elderly poor with those of public agency personnel who serve them. The authors found that services offered in a part of Los Angeles County were not particularly relevant for the elderly clients. The study data showed that a chasm existed between what the urban elderly poor perceive as necessary in services and what the public agency representatives perceive as desirable. To insure that social service programs do not fall short of success in their purpose, the authors recommended that services should begin to reflect the desired life styles of the elderly poor rather than an imposed, isolated set of bureaucratic service values.

One last illustration, a survey of public housing tenants, demonstrates the existence of the mismatch. Previous studies of public housing tenants had stressed the pathological world they inhabit, pointing to the many problem families who allegedly sought help with obtaining ostensibly much-needed social services, who cried out for day care, who had urgent needs for food, jobs, and money. The researchers found something entirely different, that

> only a handful of the almost 2,000 tenants we interviewed cited difficulties with obtaining social services. And they like their housing. Despite a litany of potential ills ranging from defective screens to leaky roofs, most said their housing was adequate and rated the management in positive terms. Few felt trapped in public housing, and most tenants regarded themselves as effective and useful human beings, mothers, and spouses.
>
> But they wanted police protection. More than anything else, they wanted security for themselves and their possessions.

What these poor tenants wanted was more security, not an elaborate social services information and referral program, which the professionals had recommended to meet the "needs" of the tenants.

We feel certain that others have uncovered similar examples of the mismatch in their own studies, and that these illustrations are the tip of a large iceberg.

Summary

So we are back to a question of standards, and all that different standards imply. On the values and responses of the elderly, little needs to be done in their private housing affairs. However, on the application of an objective rating scale, perhaps much could be done. Several million homes *are* in need of repair. A deteriorating stock of elderly-owned housing *does* raise serious issues for national housing policy involving not only the well-being of the elderly but also affecting millions of their tax-paying neighbors. It is not easy to resolve this difference in ways of looking at the problem. Nor is it easy to stem the level of disrepair, however defined. What we have learned, though, is that any serious discussion of national housing programs for elderly homeowners must not overlook the extent and implications of a needs/preferences mismatch.

PART THREE

What Next?

7

What's in the Way?

> The fundamental notion that governments should
> intervene in the social condition of aging persons
> has been firmly established in industrialized
> societies. . . .
>
> Yet, accompanying the growing commitment of
> modern societies to public intervention for the
> solution of social problems is a deepening sense of
> despair over our seeming incapacity to intervene
> effectively.
>
> Robert H. Binstock and Martin A.
> Levin in *The Political Dilemmas of In-*
> *tervention Policies*

BINSTOCK AND LEVIN correctly pinpoint a growing recognition that government intervention to solve social problems
has met with uneven success; that, in fact, "you can't solve
social problems by throwing money at them." We have, for
several reasons, been generally unable to alleviate conditions
that are defined as problems. In some instances, we do not
understand the social processes in which we try to intervene.
In others, we encounter problems of implementation and
competing objectives. Scholars and practitioners of public
policy have paid considerable attention to these obstacles.

Far less attention has been paid to a different problem,
namely, many social programs offer services that are not
desired by those who are to be helped. Where program par-

ticipation has been voluntary, the "target population" has often chosen not to get involved. Where participation has been compulsory, people have often been unreceptive to the services and thus derive few or no benefits from them.

It would be both foolish and politically infeasible to base public policies solely on the wishes of those to be helped. However, it is equally foolish, and usually dooms a program to failure, to ignore the preferences of those "in need." Therefore, our suggestions flow, in part, from the opinions and behaviors of the elderly themselves.

Public concern and spending on the elderly will remain a high national priority and be the subject of an intensifying debate. Recall that older Americans own more than nine million homes, which is more than one-fifth of the owner-occupied housing stock. Both these figures will increase during the remainder of this century. The maintenance and conservation of this stock of housing is potentially an issue of growing public awareness, along with the importance attached to the physical and financial well-being of the old folks who live in these homes. To date it is fair to say that elderly homeowners have been the forgotten object of national housing policy, although growing interest in their well-being is evidenced in bigger budget requests, recent state legislation, and the voluntary efforts of a number of private community organizations. Many advocates for the aging argue for more extensive public programs to help low-income elderly homeowners remain independent in their own homes as long as possible, a laudable goal. But it is easier to propose solutions than successfully attain socially desirable goals. To this end, it will be helpful to examine past and present programs that have focused on elderly homeowners to prevent repetition of costly mistakes. And we must take care that any suggestions or programs put forth to aid "old folks at home" take into account the preferences and wishes of the elderly themselves.

Is Government Intervention Warranted?

It is typical to find in the description of any government program wording that justifies public involvement and spending on behalf of a particular "needy" group. Although we do not see any immediate prospect of a national program to assist elderly homeowners with maintenance of their homes, property tax relief is partially presumed to free up funds for this purpose. Still, recent years have witnessed a shift away from emphasizing expensive new construction to achieve national housing targets to the presumably more economical approach of rehabilitation, renovation, and conservation of existing housing. Neighborhood restoration is now considered as important, if not more important, than new construction, especially in central cities and older suburban communities where elderly homeowners reside. Since more than half of the elderly live in pre-World War II vintage homes, growing national interest in neighborhood preservation potentially affects the majority of older home-owning Americans.

This shifting emphasis from new construction to conservation is part and parcel of the dramatic recent increase in housing costs, especially for new home buyers in several metropolitan areas. But there is also growing concern that widespread deterioration in our towns and cities will impose large social and financial costs on society as reflected both in the quality of life and the price of demolishing or rehabilitating these communities—more than half a million structures are scrapped each year. Perhaps it can be cheaper to maintain many of these homes in the short run than to rehabilitate or demolish them in the long run. As the man in the oil-filter advertisement says, "You can either pay me a little bit now or a lot later."

Is there a rationale for government intervention in the private housing and neighborhood affairs of older

137

Americans, so many of whom live in declining older cities? Supporters of intervention offer several justifications. One that is frequently cited is the 1949 Housing Act, which sets forth the goal of "a decent home and a suitable living environment for every American family." This congressional declaration is taken to reflect the will of the majority, thus enjoying legitimacy. Provision of decent housing for all citizens is a watchword of national policy, even in the absence of agreement on what it means. Some housing analysts claim that private housing markets fail to house the poor, minorities, and the elderly satisfactorily, in decent units at prices they can afford to pay. Only the government can fill this alleged gap.

Housing experts and planners can also justify publicly imposed standards of upkeep and programs for required maintenance on grounds of what they call externalities or neighborhood effects. Zoning, building codes, health and sanitation codes, and other public safety ordinances rest on the implicit claim that noise, rubbish, nuisances, or general misuse of land and property in a residential neighborhood warrant public control over private land use. Henry J. Aaron explains this externality effect in his book *Shelter and Subsidies: Who Benefits from Federal Housing Policies?*

> Even if no one cared about his neighbors' opulence or squalor, each person would probably feel the effect of others' investment in and consumption of housing services. Pride or shame about the general appearance of a neighborhood or town may induce such public actions as zoning regulations to compel each family to take into account the effects on others of its outlays on housing. . . . The conviction . . . that housing is a problem to be settled publicly must somehow reflect the impact of each family's housing on others.

If bad housing harmed not only its immediate tenant but also the immediate neighborhood in which the home was located, then a plausible case might be made for corrective public action.

We might restate this externalities or "neighborhood effects" argument another way. Deterioration does not affect just any one particular home, it presumably also affects other homeowners in a neighborhood whose incentive to maintain their homes in good condition declines as the neighborhood in which they live runs down. We live in a world in which one person's decision to invest in home maintenance affects both the value of his neighbor's house and the attractiveness of his immediate neighborhood as well. Anyone who has tried to sell his home, however well maintained, when his neighbors' homes are in bad condition understands this phenomenon. Extensive investment in any one home can lift the value of surrounding homes; conversely, one very run-down home lowers the value of neighboring properties. The same principle applies in general: It may be rational not to invest in maintaining your own home and leave property improvement to your neighbors, since any investment by a neighbor secures a free benefit for yourself.

Why, then, would any individual homeowner incur the costs of home and neighborhood improvement by himself, especially if he lives in what potential buyers perceive as a deteriorating area? Each homeowner is equally likely to reach this conclusion and wait for his neighbors to act. However, if each homeowner were required to maintain his home at some agreed-upon minimum standard, everyone in the neighborhood would live in a safer dwelling and enjoy a more pleasant environment. A policy of mandatory neighborhood preservation might, in this rationale, contribute to the continued independence and well-being of the elderly in their own homes.

If it may be rational for each individual homeowner to forgo maintenance on his home, especially in a declining neighborhood, the consequences of these individual decisions are not socially desirable since the future costs of rehabilitation, borne by society at large, may substantially exceed the present cost of maintenance. Moreover, if the home deteriorates too far, the elderly resident may be forced out of his home, surely an undesirable outcome. Might it not be better to facilitate the provision of a minimum standard of maintenance for those elderly homeowners who cannot keep their houses in good condition than to undertake significant rehabilitation in the future or risk having to arrange alternative public accommodation for these persons?

However, even if we accepted the externalities thesis and possessed a workable program of assistance to old folks in need, we still question the desirability of mandatory participation because of neighborhood effects. Compulsion is almost inherently inconsistent with independence. A program that rested on voluntary participation would avoid casting this moral issue into the forefront of debate.

We recognize that such programs as housing code enforcement are mandatory. Indeed, some localities (including Dayton) have mounted intensive housing inspection efforts for purposes of code enforcement. However, any attempt to force elderly homeowners to conform to a local (or national) housing standard in the name of helping them would certainly meet overwhelming political opposition.

An Inventory of Programs

It is not necessary to start from scratch in thinking about public or private efforts to help the aged with some of the problems they have. Quite a few elderly homeowners know about and have participated in one or more public programs that are directed at housing rehabilitation and neighborhood stabilization. For some time, both federal and state governments have sponsored several different kinds of programs.

Major rehabilitation grant and loan programs. The Department of Housing and Urban Development (HUD) has sponsored two categories of financial assistance that would enable elderly homeowners to refurbish their homes. One of these is a rehabilitation grant (technically called Section 115, since largely converted into the community development block grants program in 1975), which is an outright grant of money, and the other is a rehabilitation low-interest loan (Section 312) that must be repaid. Recipients of these grants and loans are typically poor, live in code-enforcement or urban renewal areas, and often have potential or existing code violations that need correction. These programs are not reserved exclusively for aged persons. The funding level in fiscal year 1979 authorized up to ten thousand loans, though in the preceding several years the government contracted fewer than half that number. Each annual budget has authorized more funds than the government has been able to loan. It will come as no surprise that the grant program is more popular than the loan program.

Federal community block grant funds are another major source of support for home repairs. Boston's Housing Improvement Program for older Bostonians illustrates this kind of city effort: Cash rebates of 50 percent on housing improvements are given to homeowners 65 and over who live in and have held title to their property for at least one year. The improvements can run to $15,000 for a six-family dwelling with a possible rebate of up to $7,500. Homeowners with incomes as high as $16,000 of net taxable income are eligible. All work undertaken through the rebate program must be in accordance with state building, sanitary, and fire codes. Owners are encouraged to use these funds to insulate and improve their electrical, plumbing, and heating units, as well as exterior surfaces. The chief goal of the Boston program is to stabilize neighborhoods and prevent the erosion of property values and morale.

Another example of the major loan programs is the Section 504 Home Repair Loan Program of the Farmers Homes Administration (FHA). Until fiscal year 1976, it provided low-interest loans of from $2,500 to $3,500 to homeowners in towns of ten thousand or less population. These loans carried a modest 1 percent interest rate and a repayment period of up to ten years. Curiously, the program was not widely used. In fiscal year 1973, for example, only $4.5 million of the $10 million allocation was actually spent; only $4.3 million of a similar 1974 allocation was spent.

Since 1977, eligibility has been extended to homeowners in towns of twenty thousand or less, is limited to the elderly, and the maximum loan is now $5,000. As well, outright grants can be made in place of or in addition to loans; 3,183 grants worth $10 million were made in 1978. But actual outlays continue to run at less than the authorized level. In fiscal years 1977 and 1978, just under $5 million was loaned each year; approximately 1,800 loans were contracted. Fiscal year 1979 contained the very impressive projection of $24 million, which, on past history, is an overambitious projection. Studies show that most rural persons past 65 make few improvements in their housing. Most FHA loans are used to install modern toilet facilities, repair roofs, or make major structural improvements. To be eligible means that the applicant must live in "hazardous" housing and be unable to obtain credit from other sources.

Minor housing repair programs. A number of communities have set up small repair programs best known as "chore service" or "Handy Andy" to repair steps, roofs, railings, and plumbing that the elderly cannot do themselves. Generally these programs provide up to a few thousand dollars worth of work and are financed through the state and local grants program of Title III of the Older Americans Act or state government monies. Some programs arrange for and pay contractors, or hire craftsmen to do the work, many of whom are retired elderly craftsmen.

Non-housing federal programs. Several other federal programs help with home repairs, though not as their major mission. Public service training manpower programs pay for labor and materials costs on home repair work for the elderly. Some Neighborhood Youth Corps summer programs also do small chore projects for old folks at home.

State tax relief programs. Compared with the millions of dollars that subsidize low-income elderly renters, federal spending on home repair is minuscule. Most benefits for elderly homeowners consist of state property tax relief programs, not federal loans or grants. All fifty states and the District of Columbia field programs to reduce the property tax burden on low-income elderly households, an annual benefit surpassing $2 billion. In a document entitled *Property Tax Relief Programs for the Elderly*, published by the Department of Housing and Urban Development, detailed benefits are itemized for 1974. State circuit-breaker programs disbursed nearly $500 million in benefits to 3.2 million claimants, with an average relief payment of $143. Homestead exemptions, the other major program type, distributed more than $1 billion in benefits to at least 6.3 million claimants, with the average benefits of $173.* Reasons for these state programs are to shield low-income households from large tax burdens, to slow neighborhood deterioration, and to enable the elderly to retain their own homes. The report does not recommend a federal property tax relief program in place of those administered by the states. It does note that states and localities are likely to continue and increase these benefits for the ever-growing number of older homeowners.

---

* A homestead exemption removes from taxation a stipulated dollar amount of the assessed value of homes, a sum that varies from $1,000 in Indiana to $20,000 in Hawaii. The value of benefits is thus equal to the dollar amount of the exemption multiplied by the nominal tax rate used by the taxing jurisdiction. Circuit breakers, on the other hand, vary with income levels of eligible claimants. A household is relieved of a portion of tax liability exceeding either some percentage of income, called a "threshold formula," or a "percentage of tax liability," which homeowners at each income level are expected to pay.

143

Some states and localities employ the device of "freezing taxes," which limits the dollar amount of the homeowner's tax liability to the amount he paid on that same property at age 65. Some grant a "tax deferral" in which a homeowner defers all or part of his property taxes until the property is sold or until he dies, and gives the taxing jurisdiction a lien on his house in the value of the accumulated deferred taxes, including, in some instances, compound interest. This amount is then secured from the proceeds of the sale of the property or, in the event of the owner's death, from the heirs to the property.

As we traveled through the country talking with the elderly, we conducted an extensive search for home repair programs, both in the seven sample locations and elsewhere in the nation. Altogether we investigated eighty-five programs earmarked specifically for elderly home repair, of which thirty-one were in the seven survey locations. We conducted this search in order to distill a picture of what makes for a successful program and what does not. As well, we could ask our old folks, the subject of this book, if they know of, participated in, or had any opinions about the good and bad points of available community programs.

Program Success and Failure

What makes for a successful program? Given the wide array of situations in which the elderly live, no single program stands out as the "best" possible approach to assist the aged. Although no magic formula insures success, we did uncover several community plans that enjoyed widespread esteem as evidenced by their waiting list of applicants. In several instances they had effectively addressed one of two issues of program design.

One concern of the elderly stands out—old folks are sensitive about housing inspections. They fear being compelled to undertake costly repairs to comply with codes, repairs they may be unable to afford and which they deem inessential. Thus, the most successful programs explicitly separated housing assistance from code enforcement. This separation eliminates any risk of government coercion. Participants were repeatedly informed that a visit to their home was not connected with code enforcement, could not be a cause of condemnation, nor could it bind homeowners to use their own funds for additional work. Failure to make this separation explicit discourages many potential participants from seeking help with home repair.

Rural areas face a different problem—that of publicity and public awareness. Spread out living defeats any effort at central spacing of information centers, and media coverage is less effective than in cities. Among the successful rural programs we located, and there are a scant few, outreach was an essential component, especially if the outreach workers were themselves elderly persons. We might construe the outreach worker as the equivalent of a traveling housing counselor, with a number of houses in his caseload. He assists with information, filling out forms, arranging for contractor's estimates, and so forth.

However, successful programs are more the exception than the rule. Where they flourish, typically no more than a few hundred elderly homeowners get any kind of help. As we examined the more than eighty programs on which we collected information, the obstacles to success stood out far more clearly than the attributes of success. These obstacles fall into four different categories.

Resources.   Limited funds restrict the scope and extent of locally administered programs. With the ever-present uncertainty of future resources, most communities cannot attempt comprehensive coverage of all eligible households in their jurisdiction. Thus even successful programs reach only a small fraction of the potential recipients.

Eligibility requirements. Many programs peg their eligibility requirements to very low levels of income. As a result of recent increases in Social Security, many elderly now exceed the income limits of some home assistance programs. In principle this obstacle should be easy to eliminate. However, "needs-based" assistance should still go only to those truly unable to afford the service.

Marketing. Inadequate publicity often undermines an otherwise well-conceived program of help. Homeowners cannot sign up for benefits if they do not know about them.

Except for state or local property tax relief, most older folks we talked with could not identify any government program to help the elderly with housing maintenance. Only 40 percent knew of any local programs in their community (the figure ranged from a low of 10 percent in rural Orangeburg County to a high of 66 percent in New Ulm) and many of these persons could not actually name a specific program.

During the interview, we asked each person if he or she had heard of either of the two most prominent local assistance programs in their community. The answer was again in the minority: About 40 percent had heard of one of the two programs in their own communities. But the variation from site to site is enormous. Nearly all the ethnically homogeneous residents of New Ulm have heard of both programs in their town; conversely, large-city residents were least informed.

Actual participation in government programs is more uniform; in no site have more than 17 percent taken part; with a low of 4 percent in Orangeburg. But only 7 to 8 percent of San Francisco and Dayton residents, two major cities, have had any experience with public programs. Overall, 90 percent of our survey respondents have not taken part in any program directed at the elderly. Thus, any governmental effort to help repair elderly-owned homes would be a new experience for the great majority of old folks at home.

An "independence ethic." Federal loan programs for home renovation are a dismal flop: The Farmers Home Administration has been unable to loan out even half of its authorized loan funds or give out all of its outright grant funds. The reasons for this anomaly in federal spending are not hard to find. Many aged homeowners will not go into debt, even if it means the difference between safe and unsafe housing. Some older people fear that accepting government help may lead to the government taking away their homes. Many will not participate in any program that gives a public agency some kind of lien or claim on their home.

Evidence collected in the Experimental Housing Allowance Program, one of the largest housing studies ever conducted, shows that many low-income families assign very low priority to upgrading their housing. Even when it was in their economic interest to do so, half of the program participants did not upgrade the quality of their housing. For poor people, including many elderly, a well-maintained home may not be a high priority.

More important, many older Americans have a strong sense of pride and independence, and will not accept what they see as a handout. The elderly grew up in the early decades of this century when self-reliance was a way of life; Social Security, welfare, and federal housing programs did not exist. A lot of old folks still subscribe to this venerable philosophy and will not accept any public or private aid that smacks of charity or destroys pride and self-respect. Today's youth may not share this philosophy as they age into retirement, having grown up in a welfare state of public support and services.

Finally, many old people want to leave something to their children and grandchildren—even if this means living in a run-down home or neighborhood. They want the assets that their house represents to be left to their heirs, not to the government in exchange for a promise of lifetime maintenance. As we argue below, old people should be able to

147

choose between these options—and make that choice in the knowledge that it is in face the one they really want.

Many old people were happy to talk at length with our interviewers and minced no words in describing their feelings about public programs. Especially sharp were the opinions of Dayton's elderly residents about the town's dominant repair program.

> I think it stinks. It is wasteful.
>
> The carpetbaggers of the civil war had nothing on these guys.
>
> Housing Assistance Repair Program [Model Cities] is a big rip-off and the government doesn't give a damn.
>
> I won't participate because I'm white; it is all for the blacks.

One Pittsfield oldster reflected the values so typical of New England's small-town elderly: "I won't take a loan because I don't want to leave any debts when I go."

We gave each elderly respondent in our survey ample opportunity to evaluate existing programs and measures in his community; we also explored each respondent's preferences for some kind of potential program that he might find useful. We asked the following specific question: "What kinds of programs, if any, do you think the government should set up that would be of greatest help to homeowners like yourself to repair and maintain your home?"

Replies encompassed a wide variety of suggestions. The single most popular type was tax reductions for elderly homeowners (14 percent). Tax reductions ought to be very popular for the simple reason that each homeowner would be free to spend that additional income anyway he pleases— it is not necessarily tied to spending on the home. Other replies pointed to subsidized loans (7 percent), price controls on repair contractors (8 percent), or direct government provision of home repair services (12 percent).

Of greater interest is the fact that nearly one-third of all respondents said they could not (or would not) suggest any program. Another 15 percent said (sometimes in rather emphatic language) that government should not be involved in home repair programs. Thus, just under half of all surveyed homeowners either oppose government help for home repair or have no thoughts on the subject at all.

It is informative to read through a cross section of the replies we received. More graphic remarks were elicited from the question on potential government programs than from virtually every other question put together in the entire 108-page interview schedule. Residents of Dayton achieved the high-water mark in their caustic replies.

I would like to see less government control; knock out the giveaway programs

Do away with bureaucracy and reduce taxes.

I wish the government would stay out of our affairs and people could manage their own affairs.

Cut back on inflation; there are too many giveaway programs.

Never expected any help so I haven't got any idea.

Better off with less government. People do better on their own.

Government should take all this money that is being wasted and give it to people who need it. It always goes to some welfare people who never worked in their life.

I can do better myself than I can with government.

Old taxpayers who have saved shouldn't have to pay for the ones who were just lazy all of their lives.

Never needed any help from Uncle Sam. I work and pay my own bills.

People should take care of their own and do a good job. Uncle Sam should stay out of it. The same people need help all their life in most cases. Don't save and expect too much!

Government wants too much. Better if it stays out.

Whatever the government does, we got to pay for anyway.

Wouldn't be interested in seeing any set-up. Money for programs is not used for what it is appropriated for.

See that older people don't go to nursing homes—put welfare men to work on the repairs instead of being on the dole.

These sentiments are not unique to Dayton. In New Ulm, for instance, most folks take pride in their personal independence and responsibility.

Just lower taxes and the government doesn't have to worry about maintaining your home.

I can't think of any programs but it would really help if the government officials and workers would stop asking for an increase in pay. It only makes our tax load heavier. The government should stop spending so much.

The government wastes too much money on its programs.

The government has too many programs. More people could take care of themselves if they were let alone and knew they had to.

The government should stay out of this. There is too much control from the federal government now already. We should help ourselves more locally.

One Orangeburg resident thought that the best thing would be "for the government to get completely out of their affairs and stay out." A retired Philadelphian allowed as how "any government program gets into a big mess," a view shared by several persons in Pittsfield.

You don't get anything for nothing—I'd rather be on my own.

Don't believe government should set up anything—only leads to more taxes.

Self-reliance was also a dominant theme among elderly Bay Area residents.

Never gave it a thought. I'm from the old stock—if you have nothing, you do without. If you have a dime, save a nickel. It's hard for me to understand why people can't put something away. It's up to the individual.

It's up to the individual. I think you have to help yourself.

Last, but not least, were the elderly respondents of Tulsa.

I feel the government doesn't owe us anything. Everybody wants a handout.

Keep as far away from government programs as possible.

I'm from the old school—don't believe government should interfere.

Quit throwing out money to the four winds. Balance the budget.

Any program of homeowner assistance requires some amount of cooperation from the elderly. Not only must an aged resident believe his home needs some repair that he cannot do on his own, he must also know about any program in his community for which he might be eligible. Beyond this, he must believe that his participation in the program is a "proper" activity and that he will be better off having participated. Without these requirements the voluntary involvement of elderly homeowners in such programs will continue to be limited.

151

Nearly half of the old folks suggested that some version of government assistance might be of help to themselves. However, a large minority emphatically rejects the idea of any government intervention into their private housing affairs—they live by a code of self-reliance. In some ways this is a blessing—they are not dependent on others or society for their well-being. In other ways, this ethic is a potential barrier to any public program that might seek to arrest housing decline for those who may need and want help but are too proud to ask. In the final chapter we look at a range of possible measures that might be taken to improve the well-being of the aged homeowner. As we do so, we shall consider the implications of the mismatch and the large-scale presence of an "independence ethic."

8
What's To Be Done?

CONVENTIONAL WISDOM HAS IT that many old folks need a good deal of assistance from others to get on in life. Proponents of this view often characterize the elderly as frail, helpless, or immobile. On this view one can advocate and justify numerous programs and agencies to deliver services to the elderly. The professional housing analyst, social worker, or public official identifies the needs of the elderly and, within the limits of available budgetary resources, tries to meet those needs. However, when "needs" are defined in the absence of preferences, a paternalistic view of concern may contribute to a culture of dependence.

We think it important to correct—if possible, eliminate—this wrongheaded view of older Americans by a thorough and accurate recounting of the facts of older living. When we give the elderly a chance to speak, many tell us about the importance of the homespun virtues of pride, self-reliance, and freedom of choice. From their perspective, the majority of older people neither need nor desire assistance from government officials.

Of course there remain minority categories of elderly people who desire and need assistance: the physically handicapped, the very poor, and those who have little or no information about available options. To this group the efforts of public and private agencies should be directed. But we must take care not to confuse or equate the small minority of elderly homeowners in need of subsidized help with the vast majority who maintain their independence.

Background to Action

To us, the aged are just like younger people, except that they have lived longer. We should therefore treat them as we treat everyone else with similar problems.

A focus on age per se, reaching the magic birthday of 60 or 65, has distorted our perceptions of most older Americans. We have come to feel that the aged can no longer fend for themselves, make sound decisions, or necessarily be responsible for decisions they have made or will make.

We know that most are reluctant to give up their homes and their independence. Many are also reluctant to spend equity in their homes, preferring to bequeath it to their heirs.

Who would quarrel with these values? Still, independence and self-support go hand in hand. If the elderly want or have to make housing repairs, they should rely on their own resources to the maximum degree, as should we all. Any government program subsidizing elderly-owned homes that overlooked the resources and abilities of aged people to take care of themselves and their homes on their own would constitute an unfounded transfer of resources to the elderly. It would simultaneously reinforce the conventional account of old folks in need.

The point is that the aged do not merit special government treatment simply because they are old. Some may warrant special treatment because, like the needy of all age groups, they may be poor, sick, immobile, or otherwise disadvantaged. To be retired is not, on its own, to be needy.

Many studies of the elderly call for action and propose extensive government programs to alleviate their problems. We do not share this approach. "Problems" are rarely as unambiguous as they are depicted, large-scale government programs often fail to achieve their goals, and our capacity to evoke fundamental changes in the lives of a particular target population is usually limited. Accordingly, our proposals to assist the elderly are quite modest.

Several important principles guide the formulation of our proposals. First, any program must be conceptually and administratively simple. In our federal system of government, the implementation of complex programs is often bogged down by difficulties of coordination, accountability, and conflicting objectives among the agencies and clients involved.

Second, any new government program must not be too expensive. For the foreseeable future, government will have to live increasingly with tight fiscal constraints. We have recently witnessed the first instances of widespread opposition to the expanding costs of the Social Security system. Congress already finds it difficult to pass legislation required to ensure the future viability of the system and would surely resist any new costly program to aid only a portion of the elderly.

Third, the individual choices of each elderly American are important. We firmly believe that any public effort to override substantially the spending preferences of elderly homeowners is doomed to failure (and is ethically unjustifiable as well). Since uniform agreement on the characteristics of a "decent home" does not exist, it is perhaps most sensible to let each homeowner define that concept for himself. We can justify limiting the free choices of elderly homeowners only in the presence of true neighborhood externalities or given a threat to their own health and safety. Building codes, housing codes, and zoning ordinances represent local decisions to limit the housing choices of residents. We see no reason to impose further limitations.

If we can help the elderly convert their assets into spending power as they themselves wish, then we have promoted individual choice. In this vein, we must distinguish between those who simply cannot afford to maintain their homes and those who have the economic capacity to do so, but lack an available mechanism by which to convert their assets (including home equity) into spending power. As we have argued, this latter group should not be given financial aid.

It is surely desirable that older homeowners be able to make intelligent decisions about the upkeep of their houses. Most of what we have termed the needs/preferences mismatch can be seen as a clash in values between the standards of our sample and those of experts. Still, some occupants may not perceive a potential threat to health or safety. If it is possible to inform the elderly about these threats without forcing them to pay for improvements, then the elderly will certainly be no worse off and will enjoy the benefit of knowledge by which they can, of their own free choice, make improvements.

Prescriptions for Elderly Homeowners

A quick review of our major findings is in order. First, some half of the homes we surveyed have a "critical defect," which is the absence of some minimum essential feature or the presence of a threat to health or safety. But, second, most of these defects are not seen as problems by their owners. And, third, only about one-tenth of the homes we sampled have a critical defect and are owned by poverty-level families (taking assets into account). These needy homeowners are disporportionately located in our rural site. In the urban areas, only 5 percent fall into this category. Finally, the concern that the elderly most forcefully volunteer (in this study and others) is the threat of crime in their neighborhood.

Where do the principles we have enunciated and the findings of our study lead us? In this section we outline a small number of recommendations that address the problems we have identified and conform with our notions of good public policy. There are three goals embedded in these prescriptions. First, elderly homeowners should be able to use the assets they have as they see fit. Second, they should be able to make informed choices about the maintenance and upkeep of their homes. Finally, those who are truly needy should be helped in the ways they most prefer. With these goals in mind we turn to our recommendations.

Reverse annuities. A reverse annuity, also known as a reverse mortgage, opens up a new source of income for millions of Americans whose largest source of wealth—the equity in their homes—sits idle. Reverse annuities simultaneously allow the aged to remain independent in their own homes and enjoy additional income. Using his home as collateral, the homeowner borrows money from a bank or savings institution. Monthly checks are then sent to the borrower for the rest of his life or occupancy of that home.

But the principal and the interest on the loan are not repaid monthly as in conventional mortgage loans; instead, the lender is repaid when the house is sold or its owner dies. Any money left over is paid to the owner or the heirs to the estate. In the event that the homeowner lives long enough to receive payments that exceed the value of his home, an insurance policy would guarantee continued possession.

Until 1979, government restricted federally chartered savings and loan associations and national banks in making reverse mortgages. Effective January 1, 1979, the Federal Home Loan Bank Board authorized federally chartered savings and loan associations to issue reverse-annuity mortgages; California had already permitted its state-chartered associations such loans since February 1978, preceding the national edict by nearly a year.

Reverse mortgages thus transform home equity into a stream of current income to be used for living expenses, simultaneously allowing the elderly person to continue to own his house and use it for the rest of his life.

Other Western countries follow similar practices. On January 1, 1979, France enacted a new law providing that persons 65 and over may sign over their homes to local town councils in return for a monthly remittance and the right to continue living there for the rest of their lives. The amount of the monthly check is calculated on the basis of probable life expectancy of the present owner and the property value. French policy is to enable old people to remain in their homes as long as possible.

Expand deferral of property taxes. A common story in the daily papers is the tale of the retired couple whose house is threatened by the increased taxes that have accompanied an inflation in housing assessments, especially dramatic in some communities. Although circuit-breaker and homestead provisions give some relief from property taxes, total property tax deferral can completely eliminate most of the threat rising taxes pose for home ownership. Recent California legislation is an excellent model, which the other states could profitably consider for adoption. California allows any elderly homeowner with an income below $20,000—the vast majority of aged—and with an equity of at least 20 percent in the house to defer indefinitely all property taxes; in return, the state takes a lien on the house in the amount of deferred taxes plus accumulated interest at an annual rate of 7 percent. Note that this program is not compulsory: It depends solely on the voluntary choice of each elderly household. Those who want to pass on their homes to children unencumbered by a state lien need not participate. Nor is it difficult to inform old folks of the tax-deferral opportunity; it can be clearly printed on the assessment notice or tax bill with instructions on how to get application forms. Moreover, taxes are deferred, not forgiven, so that younger property owners do not bear greater burdens.

Since property taxes rise with periodic reassessments, we propose that any elderly person who improves his home not be reassessed until after the home is sold. Some persons may postpone or forgo home improvement fearing increased property taxes. A guarantee that improvement will not mean higher taxes might encourage some elderly homeowners to make their homes safer and more comfortable. To prevent this provision from becoming a subsidy to the very rich, income or asset limits could be imposed to restrict participation to those in lower and lower-middle income groups.

Eliminate capital gains tax on the sale of an elderly-owned residence. As our survey and other data reveal, the bulk of assets that the elderly command consists of the equity in their homes. Tax relief is available for all homeowners when the sale and purchase of an equally or more expensive home is involved. Until 1978, no capital gains taxes were imposed on the profits incurred in the sale of a home for less than $35,000, and a part of the gain for a sales price over $35,000 might be excluded from gross income. However, due to inflation, property values have risen rapidly in recent years. In such communities as San Francisco many homes are worth more than $80,000. In this case and many others, the tax relief is wholly inadequate for elderly people who move from a home that they own to an apartment or to a retirement establishment of some sort. The distress is acute for many retired people who may have to consume their capital to meet inflated living expenses in the years after retirement. A reduction of capital by a capital gains tax in the year of sale of the residence is particularly harsh—expecially since the increase in value may be due chiefly to inflation and not to any real appreciation in value after inflation is taken into account.

Congress recognized these new inflationary realities. In the Revenue Act of 1978, persons aged 55 and over are entitled to exclude from taxation up to $100,000 of gains realized from the sale of a principal residence owned and occupied for three of the five years preceding the sale. California law was similarly amended. If Congress does not abolish the tax outright in future years, it should minimally index the capital gain to inflation to eliminate that part of the gain due entirely to inflation, thus restricting the tax liability to that part that is real and that exceeds the $100,000 limitation.

Encourage voluntary home inspections. Recall that housing evaluators found defects that the homeowners we talked with did not see as problems or of which they were perhaps unaware. Despite a lifetime of homeowning experience for most elderly households, some would perhaps welcome the kind of diagnosis that a housing specialist might provide.

Two conditions are vital to the success of any home inspection program. First, the inspection must be voluntary. Second, it must not impose direct liability on the homeowner for possible building or housing code violations. The elderly we interviewed were extremely sensitive to the prospective financial liability of a code violation. Indeed, our field staff took great care to guarantee that none of our survey information would be turned over to local authorities.

Private firms have recently begun to offer inspection services to the public, some of which are coupled with warranties to repair major structural and mechanical housing problems that subsequently appear. One recent study of program options sponsored by the Department of Housing and Urban Development concluded that about 5 percent of home buyers would purchase a proposed home inspection plan. This same study shows that about one-fifth of the surveyed homeowners would participate if given a subsidy of $100 to cover inspection and warranty; homeowner contributions would pay all other program costs.

These findings are preliminary but indicate that a minority of homeowners are willing to buy inspection services. They also suggest that a small subsidy might encourage others—limited to those we regard as truly needy—to participate in such a program. Although participation would not be widespread, it would be voluntary and help those who truly feel they need help in maintenance decisions (e.g., elderly widows).

Emphasize security in provision of community services. Virtually every study of the elderly we have located reveals the high priority they place on personal safety and neighborhood stability. In other words, the elderly receive less police protection than they want, and conversely perhaps more of such other services as parks, senior citizen centers, adult education classes, and nutrition centers than they require. Community decisions on the supply of local services should incorporate those views of elderly persons that emphasize security. Recall that virtually all homeowners like their homes; their chief complaint is the decline of neighborhood and personal security in recent years. A recognition of this fact by federal and local officials might prompt a reconcentration of funds spent on services for the elderly where they would be most desired.

Millions of older Americans desire to participate in the labor force on a full- or part-time basis. Some want to continue the work they have been doing for years. Others want the opportunity to supplement their income or avoid the dangers of fixed income in an inflationary period. At least two barriers restrict employment for some of these people, and we think that their removal may contribute to the independence and well-being of the elderly.

Eliminate mandatory retirement. In the past few years, several states and the federal government have enacted new laws that abolish mandatory retirement. Among the states, for example, Alaska, California, Montana, and North Carolina have prohibited age-mandated retirement in both public and private employment; other states bar age-mandated retirement either in public or private sector employment, but not both. As of January 1, 1979, federal law, with few exceptions, prohibits mandatory retirement below age 70 in private employment and in state and local government employment. The same federal statute also instructs the Secretary of Labor to study the potential elimination altogether of mandatory retirement on the basis of age.

Arguments for or against an end to age-mandated retirement abound. The case for flexible retirement argues that compulsory retirement is discrimination on the basis of age, thus violating the principle of equal employment opportunity; that age is not an accurate indicator of ability; that better utilization of the skills and experience of older workers would increase national output; that work means increased income for the aged and reduced government assistance or transfer payments to unemployed elderly; that additional employment improves life satisfaction and longevity; and that flexible retirement reduces resentment and animosity among elderly persons.

Proponents of compulsory retirement are equally forceful. They argue that compulsory retirement is easy to administer in lieu of the complicated tests that would be required to implement a program of flexible retirement; that it prevents discrimination among individuals; that it is predictable and facilitates future planning; that it reduces competition for limited jobs, especially among younger members of the work force; that it opens promotion and tenure prospects for younger workers; and that compulsory retirement precludes an older worker having to be told he is no longer capable of doing his job.

Other contentions in favor of maintaining compulsory retirement are visibly refuted by the evidence of current research. Claims that workers over 65 have impaired or declining health are not supported by studies showing that the majority of aged do not have disabling impairments or work limitations. Stereotypes that older workers are inferior and cannot adequately perform their jobs have little basis in fact. Workers who are forcibly retired after age 65 have more difficulty securing new jobs than younger men, and thus it is not easy for them to keep working just because they want to.

Abolition of age-mandated retirement does not mean that firms must retain incompetent personnel. It only means that there must be no legal status to age-determined forced retirement. Each firm or employer should reserve the right to determine the productivity of its work force of all ages and make employment decisions accordingly.

In practice, this proposal would affect some occupational groups more than others. Many factory workers already choose early retirement, which Social Security benefits or company pensions make possible. However, a minority of employees might welcome the opportunity to remain active at their jobs, and it is these people who should be given every opportunity to do so.

Repeal minimum wage laws for the elderly. The existence of minimum wage legislation makes it difficult for prospective employers to hire elderly workers. On January 1, 1976, the minimum wage stood at $2.30 per hour, having risen from $1.25 to $2.30 between 1965 and 1976. On November 1, 1977, new legislation raised the federal minimum wage to $2.65 per hour as of January 1, 1978. The law also provides for annual increases to $2.90 in 1979, $3.10 in 1980, and $3.35 in 1981. For at least two reasons, jobs are lost every time minimum wages rise. First, employers substitute skilled workers earning above the minimum wage for the below-minimum, less-skilled worker. Second, employers introduce labor-saving machinery, thereby eliminating employees whose productivity falls below the minimum wage. Those who gain from these provisions are highly skilled, often unionized workers; those who lose are the now unemployed and unemployable young, minority group members, and elderly who might be willing to work for less than the minimum wage but who are lawfully forbidden to do so.

Abolition of the minimum wage as it applies to persons aged 65 and over might open up a number of below minimum wage paying jobs for many elderly persons who cannot now find work because employers cannot afford the labor wage mandated under current law. If employers could offer below minimum wage jobs to the elderly, thousands could rejoin the labor force. Not only would a job increase the income of many elderly households, it might also reinforce the sense of pride and independence that befits the vast majority of older Americans.

Although economists assert that repeal of the federal minimum wage would mean additional jobs for many now unable to work—including elderly persons—the political acceptability of this assertion is questionable. For the same reasons that organized labor and other special interest groups want to make it difficult for employers to substitute low-cost labor for highly skilled unionized labor, they would resist repeal of minimum wages even for the elderly. However, there is no group in America for whom it is more politically attractive to offer benefits than the elderly. It would be easier, in all likelihood, to repeal minimum wages for the elderly than for any other age, ethnic-racial, or other special group.

Replace the elderly tax exemption with a credit. Currently, all aged persons over 65 may claim an extra exemption of $1,000 on their federal income tax returns. On average, this saved the elderly taxpayer about $230 in 1974. However, those who have the highest taxable incomes benefit most, while those with very low incomes benefit least. In 1974 those with adjusted gross incomes below $3,000 only received an average tax benefit of $4. Conversely, those with incomes exceeding $100,000 enjoyed an average benefit of $553.

The double exemption thus gives the greatest benefit to those least in need. We suggest, instead, that a tax credit be given to each elderly person. The size of the credit would be the same for each recipient and might be set equal to the average benefit of the current exemption. This approach would be administratively simple, not cost much more than the current exemption, and provide more help to those most in financial need.

This set of prescriptions will better enable most old folks to take care of themselves in whatever manner they choose than if government provided a package of direct services that would necessitate a large bureaucracy and the substitution of paternalism for self-reliance.

The statements of 1,575 elderly homeowners show no need for further regulation of or interference with the private market for housing services. Most users say they are satisfied with the quality and price of the services they have purchased. Regulating this market ostensibly to help elderly homeowners might well raise costs and reduce the supply of services from which elderly persons could choose.

We would be remiss if we failed to acknowledge the risk that inflation poses for independent living, raising some costs more quickly than rising Social Security benefits can restore. Removing obstacles and impediments to self-help can offset some of inflation's harmful effects. But an outright cure to inflation is a more intractable problem. Its defeat requires the government of the United States to adopt a set of responsible fiscal policies that minimize inflation. There is no painless solution to this problem, yet its importance overrides most other social issues. It seems, like death and taxes, to be becoming inevitable. Our prescriptions focus on raising elderly incomes as a direct means of coping with inflation.

The Needy Few

There remains a residual class of elderly homeowners for whom self-support and independence are noble ideals, but not everyday realities. Although we have no precise estimate of their numbers, we know they comprise fewer than 10 percent of those in urban areas, but perhaps as many as one-third in rural areas. There is no simple solution for the problems of these people.

It is, in our opinion, more important to address the poverty of these people than their housing condition. Additional money spent on food or fuel might be of greater value to them than money spent on roof repair (though that must be their judgment). We contend, then, that efforts to improve the economic well-being of poor elderly homeowners should remain a vital part of our overall policy of income maintenance that applies to all older Americans.

Nor have we resolved the issue on differences in housing standards among localities. Research on this subject suggests rural residents have lower housing standards then urban dwellers. Since housing and building codes are locally determined, it may be inappropriate to superimpose a federal standard over local communities. Those who propose federal solutions to housing problems must be sensitive to this question.

Elderly homeowners in central city neighborhoods, which have undergone substantial income and ethnic transition, face perhaps the most difficult circumstances of all. Their older houses have often declined in value compared with the rest of the local housing market. Some of these are the very same persons with critical defects in their homes, who are most likely to be unhappy with their neighborhood and the threat of crime. Yet they cannot afford to purchase better housing elsewhere in their community.

For this group of homeowners there are no easy answers. They are faced with a rising cost of living at the very time the annuity potential of their home is declining. Moreover, one must question the economic wisdom of home repair and maintenance in a physically declining neighborhood. This is the one group of elderly homeowners that may be truly "trapped" in their homes. Although we should facilitate the use of their assets, we must also realize there may be a need to do more for this relatively small number of people whose choices have been unexpectedly and involuntarily reduced.

Throughout this book we have spoken about the vast majority of the noninstitutionalized, independent elderly who are able to make choices for themselves about their lives and homes. At some point, though, some will lose this capacity because of mental or physical decline. When to acknowledge this fact and what to do about it are tough issues, but these are typically handled by family or close friends. As we have shown earlier, only a few do not have the benefit of family support. We leave to other practitioners and students of aging the task of addressing this difficult but very real issue for those few who are truly isolated and can no longer care for themselves. For them, sustained independent living is a complex task made easier by such conventionally delivered services as "meals on wheels," "homemaker/home health aides," "visiting nurses," "friendly calls," and others. Admittedly, this world of service delivery is imperfect: Many who receive services don't need them, and many in need fail to receive them.

It is all too facile to simplify a complex world, to say that we can always distinguish rational individuals from helpless, needy persons. We find it more straightforward to propose measures that benefit the great majority who are independent than the few who may require direct assistance. But when it comes to providing this assistance, the needy few are as often missed as reached, and benefits often wastefully spill over to the great numbers of those who don't need them.

Recall also the importance of the mismatch. Expert-imputed needs rarely correspond with individually held preferences. To reach that small minority for whom needs and preferences coincide requires accurate targeting and close monitoring. Appropriation of new monies for social purposes throughout the 1980s looks increasingly unlikely. Limited funds for services to the aging, perhaps even reductions, compel us not to waste services on those who neither need nor want them at the expense of those who do.

Society should continue to take care of the truly needy as best it can, rejecting panaceas promising that an imperfect world of service delivery can become perfect— or even substantially less wasteful. The important message, then, is that the dog must wag the tail, not the other way around. Drumbeating emphasis on the misfortunes of a minority of old folks must not obscure the reality of the great majority, or serve to buttress old or advocate new mistaken policies.

Appendixes

Appendix A

Sampling Procedure

IN THE STRICT LANGUAGE of sampling theory, we undertook a multi-stage, proportionate, stratified cluster sample of elderly homeowners in the five sites that qualified as Standard Metropolitan Statistical Areas. To reflect the variation in neighborhood social and economic conditions, we first stratified census tracts into three groups on the basis of tract median income: below $10,000, $10,000 to $15,000, and over $15,000. We then calculated the total number of elderly (aged 60 and over) in each tract, from which we calculated the proportions of elderly who lived in low, medium, and high income communities.

In the second stage, fifteen tracts were selected. For each tract income group, the number of tracts chosen was in proportion to the number of elderly who lived in that group. That is, if an income stratum had 40 percent of all elderly, six tracts were chosen from it (0.4 × 15 tracts = 6 tracts). Within each stratum we selected the appropriate number of tracts with probability in proportion to the number of elderly residents in each tract. For example, a tract having 750 such individuals had three times the probability of being selected as one with 250 elderly.

In the third stage, we chose five blocks within each tract. Each block was drawn with probability in proportion to the number of elderly residents living on it.

In the final stage, we selected three homes on each block, using a procedure which insured that each eligible

171

homeowner had an equal opportunity of being selected for interview. On each block, the interviewer arbitrarily chose one corner. He then counted a number (randomly selected between 0 and 5) of houses from that corner. If the owner of the home and the home itself were eligible, they were included in the sample. If not, the interviewers ascertained the location of other elderly homeowners on that block near the home and worked their way around the block, using this procedure, until they completed three interviews. If fewer than three could be completed, they were made up on alternate blocks within that tract also chosen with probability proportional to the number of elderly residents.

In sum, 225 interviews were obtained by performing 3 interviews on each block, on 5 blocks per tract, in 15 tracts ($3 \times 5 \times 15 = 225$). (Details about the two non-SMSA sites appear in the text.)

Appendix B
Housing Evaluation Form

THE HOUSING EVALUATION FORM (HEF) was developed in order to obtain reliable ratings of housing condition. It represents a revision of the instrument used in the Experimental Housing Allowance Program to measure housing standards. To insure maximum reliability among surveyors, we issued a set of instructions to each surveyor that prescribed how to rate thirty-nine different features found inside and outside of each dwelling unit. We show here two sample pages from those instructions to illustrate both conceptual matter and specific rating criteria. The manual was fifty-two pages long.

Items 7-9

These items are very similar so work carefully with the form. We are concerned about the condition of both <u>surfaces</u> and <u>structure</u> and the extent to which repairs may be required, so we have included separate questions for each item. Be certain that your evaluation is on <u>either</u> surface <u>or</u> structure, depending upon the question being evaluated. For each item, rate on the basis of the worst condition present — you will be expected to rate each of the four walls in every room as well as the ceiling and the floor. In each of these six items, you will be rating on a scale of 0-3. You will also be rating the type of material used. Be certain to read the ratings carefully. As a rule, 0 is the best rating and indicates a like-new condition. However, do not downgrade surface of structure simply because the unit is old if the element being rated is in what you consider to be like-new condition. The 3 rating indicates a need for replacement. The 1 and 2 ratings lie in between. Be certain that you have read and understand each of the different rating scores before attempting to answer questions 7-9.

173

7. Ceiling:

	LR	BTH	KCN	DNG	BDR	BDR
a. Structure	☐	☐	☐	☐	☐	☐
b. Material (If other, describe)	☐	☐	☐	☐	☐	☐
c. Surface	☐	☐	☐	☐	☐	☐

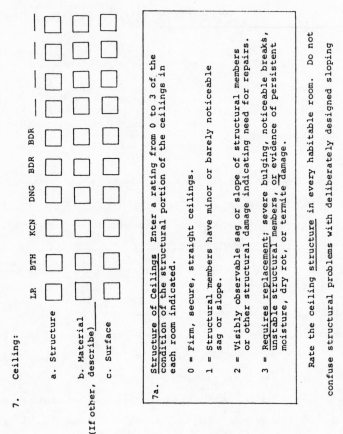

7a. **Structure of Ceilings** Enter a rating from 0 to 3 of the condition of the structural portion of the ceilings in each room indicated.

0 = Firm, secure, straight ceilings.

1 = Structural members have minor or barely noticeable sag or slope.

2 = Visibly observable sag or slope of structural members or other structural damage indicating need for repairs.

3 = Requires replacement; severe bulging, noticeable breaks, unstable structural members, or evidence of persistent moisture, dry rot, or termite damage.

Rate the ceiling structure in every habitable room. Do not confuse structural problems with deliberately designed sloping ceilings.

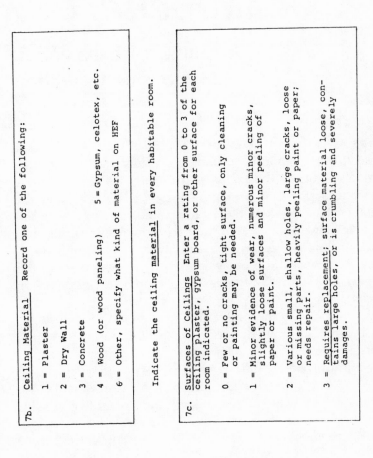

7b. Ceiling Material   Record one of the following:

1 = Plaster

2 = Dry Wall

3 = Concrete

4 = Wood (or wood paneling)   5 = Gypsum, celotex, etc.

6 = Other, specify what kind of material on HEF

Indicate the ceiling material in every habitable room.

7c. Surfaces of Ceilings   Enter a rating from 0 to 3 of the ceiling plaster, gypsum board, or other surface for each room indicated.

0 = Few or no cracks, tight surface, only cleaning or painting may be needed.

1 = Minor evidence of wear, numerous minor cracks, slightly loose surfaces and minor peeling of paper or paint.

2 = Various small, shallow holes, large cracks, loose or missing parts, heavily peeling paint or paper; needs repair.

3 = Requires replacement; surface material loose, contains large holes, or is crumbling and severely damages.

Rate the ceiling surface in every habitable room.

Appendix C

A Statistical Explanation
of Housing Condition

THIS APPENDIX ANALYZES more thoroughly the factors that lead to poor housing condition. These factors include characteristics of the elderly homeowner, his home, and his neighborhood. Our primary concern is disentangling the relationships between these factors and housing condition, but in doing so it is important to recognize the reciprocal relationship between wealth and housing condition. Therefore, we concentrate on what statisticians call a structural model, which we estimate using multivariate regression techniques.

We note at the outset that this exercise is partly exploratory. No single theoretical model of housing condition has been developed by economists, and few empirical studies specifically address this issue. Also, as with virtually all studies of housing markets, there are some variables we would like to include in the analysis but do not (e.g., the income of neighborhood residents). On the other hand, we have considered some variables (e.g., wealth and health of the owner) that have not, to our knowledge, appeared in any other study.

The structure of our model consists of two equations, which are outlined in the accompanying figure. One equation predicts the value of each respondent's home (Y_1). The second equation, the focus of our interest, predicts the condi-

A Simple Structural Model of Housing Condition

$$Y_1 = f(X_1, X_2, X_3, X_4, X_5, X_6, X_7, X_8, X_9, X_{10}, Y_2)$$
$$Y_2 = g(X_2, X_5, X_6, X_7, X_8, X_9, X_{10}, X_{11}, X_{12}, X_{13}, X_{14}, X_{15}, X_{16}, Y_1)$$

where:

Y_1 = value of home (the analysis included only those who own their homes free and clear; thus value of home is equal to home equity)

Y_2 = housing condition (number of systems with critical defects)

X_1 = neighborhood race (perception of homeowner measured on a five-point scale from "all white" to "all nonwhite")

X_2 = age of house

X_3 = number of rooms in house

X_4 = number of bathrooms in house

X_5 to X_{10} = dummy variables for six sites (excluding Orangeburg)

X_{11} = age of homeowner

X_{12} = race of homeowner (black = 1, others = 0)

X_{13} = education of homeowner (years of schooling)

X_{14} = health of homeowner (self-reported on a four-point scale from "poor" to "excellent")

X_{15} = current income of owner

X_{16} = wealth of owner (assets other than equity in the home)

tion of each home (Y_2). In verbal terms, we say that the value of a home is a function (f) of the characteristics of the people in the neighborhood;* characteristics of the home (its age, number of rooms, number of bathrooms, its condition); and the housing market in which it is located. In turn, the condition of the home is a function (g) of the age of the home; the housing market in which it is located; noneconomic characteristics of the homeowner (his age, race, education, and health); and the economic status of the homeowner (current income, home equity, and other assets).

We asked each respondent to estimate what price he could get if he sold his home. The responses were used to measure the value of the home. Other studies have shown this procedure provides a good estimate of housing value. Since we included only those homes that were owned

---

* In this case we used race of people in the neighborhood. We would have preferred to use both income and race, but did not have income figures for all seven sites.

outright, the estimate of housing value is equivalent to an estimate of equity in the home.

Since the condition of the home is assumed to depend partially on the value of the home, while the value depends partially on the condition, we have a simultaneous relationship. Thus, ordinary least squares regression analysis is inappropriate, and we rely upon two-stage least squares analysis in the estimation of the equations.

Recall that many of our respondents refused to answer some of the questions about their assets. In Chapter 3 we tested the sensitivity of our estimates of economic well-being by doing the analysis three times: for those who answered all questions about wealth and income, for those who refused to answer no more than one question on either wealth or income, and for those who refused to answer no more than two questions about wealth or income. We used a similar procedure here, estimating our structural models three times.

The table presents the estimation of the second equation predicting condition of home (for those respondents who refused to answer no more than one question about income or wealth). We should note that, with one exception, those coefficients significant in this equation are also significant in the two other estimations (for those with none or up to two refusals on financial questions). For the exception (equity in the home) the coefficient is insignificant in only one equation.

Let us review the results. We find that older homes, homes owned by blacks, and those owned by people who see themselves in poor health are all in worse shape. Homes in Orangeburg County have more critical defects than those at other sites. The age and education of an owner seem not to have a direct effect on the condition of his home.

The coefficients for current income, equity in the home, and other assets are all negative, with only the second statistically significant.

Regression Analysis of Housing Condition
(Dependent Variable: Number of Systems with Critical Defects)

Independent Variable	Regression Coefficient	Standard Error of the Coefficient	Statistical Significance
Age of house	.0093	.0027	p < .001
Age of owner	.0049	.008	N.S.[a]
Education of owner	−.019	.022	N.S.
Race of owner[b]	1.40	.301	p < .001
Health of owner	−.158	.070	p < .01
Income[c]	−.053	.044	N.S.
Wealth (excluding equity)[c]	−.0019	.023	N.S.
Equity (predicted)[c]	−.513	.266	p < .10
Philadelphia[d]	−1.79	.30	p < .001
San Francisco[d]	−1.22	.41	p < .01
Dayton[d]	−1.16	.27	p < .001
Pittsfield[d]	−1.79	.33	p < .001
Tulsa[d]	−1.56	.24	p < .001
New Ulm[d]	−1.65	.27	p < .001
Constant	6.97		

$R^2 = .47$, $F = 39.34$
mean = 1.44
[a] not significant (p ≥ .10)
[b] black = 1, other = 0
[c] variable in log form
[d] relative to Orangeburg

We must interpret the coefficients with caution. The co-efficient for equity indicates that those who have more assets in their homes have higher housing quality. However, assets held as equity in the home are highly correlated with assets held in other forms. The average correlation between the two variables (across the three samples) is .69. The correlations between income and equity and other assets are somewhat lower, averaging .41 and .45 respectively.

To assess the total impact of economic status we tested the null hypothesis that all of the three coefficients were the same and equal to 0. We may reject this hypothesis ($F_{2,620}$ 4.29, $p < .025$). Thus the financial well-being of the homeowner does affect the condition of the house.

We also tested the hypothesis that assets held as equity in the home have the same effect as assets held in other forms. This is also rejected, though at a lower level of statistical significance ($F_{1,621} = 3.36$, $p < .10$). We find no significant differences between the coefficients for equity and current income, or between those for income and other assets.

Each of these results held for at least two of the three sets of equations we estimated.

Notes

Chapter 1. Facts and Fallacies on Aging
(pp. 3–18)

3. *$112 billion estimate:* Joseph A. Califano, Jr., "U.S. Policy for the Aging—A Commitment to Ourselves," in *National Journal*, September 30, 1978, p. 1575.

3. *Califano projection:* Robert B. Hudson, "Political and Budgetary Consequences of an Aging Population," in *National Journal*, October 21, 1978, p. 1699.

3. *40 percent estimate:* Joseph A. Califano, Jr., *op. cit.*, p. 1576.

3. *second* Time *story: October 10, 1977.*

4. New Republic *story:* December 2, 1978.

4. National Journal *story:* October 28, 1978.

4. *living arrangements percentages:* Irving R. and Miriam Dickman, *Where Older People Live: Living Arrangements for the Elderly*, Public Affairs Pamphlet No. 556 (New York: Public Affairs Committee, March 1978).

5. *home ownership figures:* derived from *1973 Annual Housing Survey, Part A, General Housing Characteristics*, Series H–150–73A, Table A–1 (page 3), *1970 Census of Housing, Housing of Senior Citizens*, Table A–8 (page 11); and *1970 Census of Housing, United States Summary*, Table 1 (page 9).

5. *1967 poverty level figures:* Robert C. Atchley, *The Social Forces in Later Life: An Introduction to Social Gerontology* (Belmont, Calif.: Wadsworth, 1972), p. 139.

5. *U.S. Senate figures:* Robert N. Butler, *Why Survive? Being Old in America* (New York, Harper & Row, 1975), p. 24.

5. *Administration on Aging figures:* Bert Kruger Smith, *Aging in America* (Boston: Beacon, 1973), pp. 53–54. The original figures appear in *Facts & Figures On Older Americans: Income and Poverty in 1970—Advance Report*, Administration on Aging, Department of Health, Education and Welfare, DHEW Publication No. (OHD/AoA) 73–20183, June 1971.

6. *Annual Housing Survey figures: 1973 Annual Housing Survey, Part C, Financial Characteristics of the Housing Inventory*, Series H–150–73C, p. xv.

6. *health statistics:* John K. Iglehart, "The Cost of Keeping the Elderly Well," in *National Journal*, October 28, 1978, pp. 1728–29.

6. *85 percent estimate:* Jon Hendricks and C. Davis Hendricks, *Aging in Mass Society: Myths and Realities* (Cambridge, Mass.: Winthrop, 1977), p. 174.

6. *activity limitation estimates: Current Estimates from the Health Interview Survey: United States—1973*, U.S. Department of Health, Education and Welfare, DHEW Publication No. (HRA) 75–1522, October 1974, Table 9.

6. *1970 Census of Housing figures: 1970 Housing of Senior Citizens*, Table A–4 (p. 6).

6. *housing value estimates:* comparison derived from Table A–4 of the *1970 Housing of Senior Citizens* and Table A–1 of the *1973 Annual Housing Survey, Part A*.

7. *overhousing thesis:* Bernard Benjamin Hoffman, Jr., *Forced Home Ownership* (Syracuse, N.Y.: Syracuse University, 1967).

7. *rural flush toilet estimates:* Chester Hartman, *Housing and Social Policy* (Englewood Cliffs, N.J.: Prentice-Hall, 1973), p. 10.

7. *Consumer Price Index figures: Economic Report of the President*, January 1978, Table B–49, consumer price indices by expenditure classes, 1929–77, p. 313.

7. *mobility estimates:* Herman B. Brotman, "The Aging of America: A Demographic Profile," in *National Journal*, October 7, 1978, p. 1625, and *Demographic Aspects of Aging and the Older Population in the United States*, Current Population Reports, Special Studies, Series P–23, No. 59, issued May 1976, U.S. Department of Commerce, Bureau of the Census, p. 20.

7. *causes of social isolation:* Barbara Silverstone and Helen Kandel Hyman, *You and Your Aging Parent* (New York: Pantheon, 1976), p. 76.

8. *solitary confinement quote: Let's End Isolation*, Administration on Aging, U.S. Department of Health, Education and Welfare, DHEW Publication No. (OHD) 75-20129, December 1974.

8. *employment estimates:* H. B. Brotman, *op. cit.*, p. 1623.

8. *Butler quotes:* R. N. Butler, *op. cit.*, pp. 1, 3.

9. *Butler's recommendations: Ibid., passim.*

9. *"poor" elderly estimates:* Robert J. Samuelson, "Aging America: Who Will Shoulder the Growing Burden?" in *National Journal*, October 28, 1978, p. 1714.

10. *housing values:* George Sternlieb, "The Private Sector's Role in the Provision of Reasonably Priced Housing," in *Resources for Housing*, Proceedings of the First Annual Conference (San Francisco: Federal Home Loan Bank of San Francisco, 1976), p. 211.

10. *health estimates:* Barbara Silverstone and Helen Kandel Hyman, *op. cit.*, p. 66.

10. *survey results:* Louis Harris and Associates, Inc., *The Myth and Reality of Aging in America* (Washington, D.C.: National Council on the Aging, April 1975), p. 130.

11. *Mayer quote:* Martin Mayer, *The Builders: Houses, People, Neighborhoods, Governments, Money* (New York: Norton, 1978), p. 17.

11. *improvement in housing quality:* John C. Weicher, "'A Decent Home': An Assessment of Progress Toward the National Housing Goal and Policies Adopted to Achieve it," in Donald Phares (ed.), *A Decent Home and Environment: Housing Urban America* (Cambridge, Mass.: Ballinger, 1977), p. 143.

11. *elderly-owned housing quality:* Raymond J. Struyk, *The Housing Situation of Elderly Americans* (Washington, D.C.: The Urban Institute, November 1976).

11. *property tax relief programs:* Abt Associates, Inc., *Property Tax Relief Programs for the Elderly, Final Report*, U.S. Department of Housing and Urban Development, Office of Policy Development and Research, November 1975.

11. *residential alteration estimates:* "Residential Alterations and Repairs: Expenditures on Residential Additions, Alterations,

Maintenance, and Replacements," Construction Reports
C50–74–Q1 and Q2, U.S. Department of Commerce, Social
and Economic Statistics Administration, Bureau of the Census, 1974.

11. *Harris survey:* Louis Harris and Associates, Inc., *op. cit.,*
p. 130.

11. *denial of forced overhousing:* See evidence in Chapter 3.

12. *isolation literature:* TransCentury Corporation, *Report on
the Literature Concerned with Social Isolation of the Elderly,*
draft report submitted to the Administration on Aging,
November 1974.

12. *prefer separation from children:* Barbara Silverstone and
Helen Kandel Hyman, *op. cit.,* p. 185.

12. *early retirement: Demographic Aspects of Aging,* Series
P–23, pp. 49–50.

12. *reduced benefits at early retirement:* James W. Singer, "A
Brighter Future for Older Workers," in *National Journal,* October 28, 1978, p. 1722.

14. *location of aged: Demographic Aspects of Aging,* Series,
P–23, pp. 16–23.

Chapter 2. The Aged Come of Age
(pp. 19–33)

19. *Pratt quote:* Henry J. Pratt, *The Gray Lobby* (Chicago:
University of Chicago Press, 1976), p. 11.

19. *Social Security literature:* One compendium of documents
and interpretive essays is Rita Ricardo Campbell, *Social
Security: Promise and Reality* (Stanford, Calif.: Hoover Institution Press, 1977). See also Alicia H. Munnell, *The Future
of Social Security* (Washington, D.C.: The Brookings Institution, 1977); Marshall R. Colberg, *The Social Security Retirement Test: Right or Wrong?* (Washington, D.C.: American
Enterprise Institute, 1978); and James H. Schulz, *The
Economics of Aging* (Belmont, Calif.: Wadsworth, 1976).
These few references are just the tip of an iceberg of
voluminous writing on the various features and controversies
surrounding Social Security.

20. *Goldwater campaign:* Rochelle Jones, *The Other Generation:*

The New Power of Older People (Englewood Cliffs, N.J.: Prentice-Hall, 1977), p. 222.

20. *Social Security outlays: The Budget of the United States Government, Fiscal Year 1979*, pp. 3, 36, 269.

20. *elderly births and deaths:* Herman B. Brotman, "The Aging of America: A Demographic Profile," in *National Journal*, October 7, 1978, p. 1622. See also *Demographic Aspects of Aging and the Older Population in the United States*, Current Population Reports, Special Studies, Series P–23, No. 59, issued May 1976, U.S. Department of Commerce, Bureau of the Census.

20. *population projections to 2040: Demographic Aspects of Aging*, Series P–23, p. 9.

21. *life expectancy estimates:* U.S. Dept. of Health, Education and Welfare, cited in *U.S. News and World Report*, November 7, 1977, p. 70.

21. *historical life spans:* Jon Hendricks and C. Davis Hendricks, *Aging in Mass Society: Myths and Realities* (Cambridge, Mass.: Winthrop, 1977), pp. 26–44.

22. *life expectancy in colonial America:* David Hackett Fischer, *Growing Old in America* (New York: Oxford University Press, 1977), p. 227.

22. *median age estimates:* David Hackett Fischer, *op. cit.*, p. 27.

22. *early students of aging:* Jon Hendricks and C. Davis Hendricks, *op. cit.*, pp. 17–21.

23. *Social Security Act:* Rita Ricardo Campbell, *op. cit.*, p. 3.

23. *50,000 titles:* J. Hendricks and C. D. Hendricks, *op. cit.*, p. 20.

23. *1,275 educational programs:* David Hackett Fischer, review essay in *New Republic*, December 2, 1978, p. 32.

24. *Massachusetts commission on aging:* David Hackett Fischer, *Growing Old in America* (New York: Oxford University Press, 1977), p. 157.

24. *134 federal programs:* Rochelle L. Stanfield, "Services for the Elderly: A Catch-22," in *National Journal*, October 28, 1978, p. 1718.

25. *colonial retirement practices:* David Hackett Fisher, *op. cit.*, pp. 43–44.

25. *Plymouth Colony: Ibid.*, p. 46.

25. *compulsory retirement:* Ibid., pp. 80, 142.

25. *elderly employment estimates:* Robert J. Samuelson, "Aging America: Who Will Shoulder the Growing Burden?" in *National Journal,* October 28, 1978, p. 1713.

26. *old-age dependency estimates:* David Hackett Fischer, *op. cit.,* p. 174.

26. *living arrangements: Demographic Aspects of Aging,* Series P-23, pp. 45-49.

26. *colonial living arrangements:* David Hackett Fischer, *op. cit.,* p. 56.

27. *history of old age assistance:* D. B. Bromley, *The Psychology of Human Ageing,* 2nd (Baltimore: Penguin Books, 1974), pp. 53-55.

27. *European pension programs:* David Hackett Fischer, *op. cit.,* p. 160.

28. *postwar American developments:* Paul A. Kerschner, "Changing Legislation: Its Effect on Programs," in Richard H. David (ed.), *Aging: Prospects and Issues,* Revised (Los Angeles: Ethel Percy Andrus Gerontology Center, University of Southern California, 1974), pp. 152-156. See also Henry J. Pratt, *op. cit., passim.*

28. *Older Americans Act: Older Americans Act of 1965, As Amended and Related Acts,* Administration on Aging, U.S. Department of Health, Education and Welfare, DHEW Publication No. (OHD) 75-20170, December 1974.

29. *Older Americans Act funding: Memorandum,* Special Committee on Aging, United States Senate, August 9, 1977, p. 1. *Memorandum* of February 3, 1978, reports final 1978 fiscal level at $538 million.

29. *medical program estimates:* John K. Iglehart, *op. cit.,* p. 1728.

29. *public housing figures:* Alvin Rabushka and William G. Weissert, *Caseworkers or Police? How Tenants See Public Housing* (Stanford, Calif.: Hoover Institution Press, 1977), pp. 6-10.

29. *federal outlays in aging: Facts & Figures on Older Americans, Federal Outlays in Aging, Fiscal Years 1967-72,* Administration on Aging, U.S. Department of Health, Education and Welfare, DHEW Publication No. (OHD/AoA) 74-20004, June 1971.

30. *list of programs: Memorandum*, Special Committee on Aging, United States Senate, February 3, 1978, pp. 1–2.
31. *building and housing codes:* Harry J. Wexler and Richard Peck, *Housing and Local Government: A Research Guide for Policy Makers and Planners* (Lexington, Mass.: Heath, 1975), pp. 53–60.
32. For a comprehensive list of government housing programs, see appendix in Henry Aaron, *Shelter and Subsidies* (Washington, D.C.: The Brookings Institution, 1972).

Chapter 3. The Facts on Old Folks at Home
(pp. 34–65)

35. *Louis Harris survey: The Myth and Reality of Aging in America*, conducted for The National Council on the Aging, Inc., by Louis Harris and Associates, Inc., April 1975.
35. *aging demographic sources:* Two comprehensive sources are *Demographic Aspects of Aging and the Older Population in the United States*, Current Population Reports, Special Studies, Series P-23, No. 59, issued May 1976, U.S. Department of Commerce, Bureau of the Census; and Lenore E. Bixby et al., *Demographic and Economic Characteristics of the Aged, 1968 Social Security Survey*, U.S. Department of Health, Education and Welfare, Social Security Administration, Research Report No. 45, DHEW Publication No. (SSA) 75–11802, 1975.
35. *sex composition figures: Demographic Aspects of Aging,* Series P-23, pp. 12–14.
36. *fatal illnesses:* National Center for Health Statistics, Department of Health, Education and Welfare, *Health in the Later Years*, 1971, cited in Jon Hendricks and C. Davis Hendricks, *Aging in Mass Society: Myths and Realities* (Cambridge, Mass.: Winthrop, 1977), pp. 173–75.
36. *suicides:* E. H. Powell, "Occupation, Status and Suicide: Toward a Redefinition of Anomie," in *American Sociological Review*, April 1958, pp. 131–139, and the *New York Times*, Sunday, October 8, 1967, Section IV, p. 6.
36. *marital status: Demographic Aspects of Aging,* Series P-23, pp. 28, 45, 47.

36. *Black life expectancy:* Richard S. Sterne et al., *The Urban Elderly Poor: Racial and Bureaucratic Conflict* (Lexington, Mass.: Heath, 1974), p. 2.

37. *longevity estimates:* U.S. Dept. of Health, Education and Welfare, cited in *U.S. News & World Report,* November 7, 1977, p. 70.

37. *geographic distribution: Demographic Aspects of Aging,* Series P–23, p. 16.

37. *urban-rural distribution: Ibid.,* p. 23.

39. *Dayton:* For a detailed study of housing in Dayton see Nina Jaffe Gruen and Claude Gruen, *Low and Moderate Income Housing in the Suburbs: An Analysis for the Dayton, Ohio Region* (New York: Praeger, 1972).

40. *sampling procedure:* To insure accuracy and reliability, supervisory staff in charge of the field effort conducted a 10 percent validation of the entire sample.

46. *location of elderly near children:* Ethel Shanas et al., *Old People in Three Industrial Societies* (New York: Atherton, 1968), cited in David Hackett Fischer, *Growing Old in America* (New York: Oxford University Press, 1977), p. 147.

46. *Harris survey on seeing children: The Myth and Reality of Aging in America,* p. 73.

47. *elderly prefer to live alone:* Edward Prager, "Subsidized Family Care of the Aged: U.S. Senate Bill 1161," in *Policy Analysis,* Fall 1978, pp. 481–82.

47. *elderly activities: The Myth and Reality of Aging in America,* pp. 74–75.

47. *Butler's chapter:* Robert N. Butler, *Why Survive? Growing Old in America* (New York: Harper & Row, 1975), pp. 22–36.

47. *Atchley quote:* Robert C. Atchley, *The Social Forces in Later Life: An Introduction to Social Gerontology* (Belmont, Calif.: Wadsworth, 1972), p. 139.

48. *underreporting of income:* James H. Schulz, "Income Distribution and the Aging," in Robert H. Binstock and Ethel Shanas, *Handbook of Aging and the Social Sciences* (New York: Van Nostrand Reinhold, 1976), p. 566, *Demographic and Economic Characteristics of the Aged,* p. 154, and Con-

gressional Budget Office, *Poverty Status of Families Under Alternative Definitions of Income*, Revised June 1977, p. 6.

48. *Schulz's estimates:* James H. Schulz, *op. cit.*, pp. 561–91.

48. *Census Bureau survey:* cited in Schulz, *op. cit.*, p. 564.

49. *Orshansky citation:* cited in Schulz, *op. cit.*, p. 568.

49. *Moon estimate:* Marilyn Moon, *The Measurement of Economic Welfare: Its Application to the Aged Poor* (New York: Academic Press, 1977), pp. 68–69.

50. *Congressional Budget Office estimate:* Congressional Budget Office, *ibid.*, p. 31.

50. *elderly tax benefits:* Publication 554, *Tax Benefits for Older Americans, 1978 Edition*, Department of the Treasury, Internal Revenue Service, and *New York Times*, November 9, 1978, page D16.

50. *Harris survey on money problems: The Myth and Reality of Aging in America*, p. 131.

52. *Moon's analysis:* Marilyn Moon, *op. cit.*

52. *lifetime expectancy:* National Center for Health Statistics, *Vital Statistics of the United States*, Vol. II-Section 5, Life Tables, p. 5-4.

53. *poverty line:* Congressional Budget Office, *ibid.*, p. 23.

54. *upstate New York study:* Richard S. Sterne, *op. cit.*, p. 26.

55. *Harris survey on health: The Myth and Reality*, p. 30.

56. *Urban elderly poor quote: Richard Sterne, op. cit.*, p. 1.

57. *Golden citation:* Herbert M. Golden, "Black Ageism," in *Social Policy*, November–December 1976, pp. 40–42.

57. *Dancy volume:* Institute of Gerontology, University of Michigan, 1977.

57. *Aging issue:* U.S. Department of Health, Education and Welfare, Administration on Aging. The six essays are Robert Hill, "A Demographic Profile of the Black Elderly," pp. 2–9; Jay Chunn, "The Black Aged and Social Policy," pp. 10–14; Jacquelyne Johnson Jackson, "Special Health Problems of Aged Blacks," pp. 15–20; William E. Huling, "Evolving Family Roles for Black Elderly," pp. 21–27; N. Alan Sheppard, "A Federal Perspective on the Black Aged: From Concern to Action," pp. 28–32; and Roosevelt Johnson, "Barriers to Adequate Housing for Elderly Blacks," pp. 33–39.

58. *percent of elderly homeowners black:* derived from *1973 Annual Housing Survey, Part A, General Housing Characteristics* series H–150–73–A, Table A–1 (page 3) and Table A–4 (page 17).

58. *negative stereotype quote:* Conference on *Images of Old Age in the American Media*, The American Jewish Committee, New York, December 8, 1977, p. 5.

59. *Harris survey on aging problems: The Myth and Reality*, pp. 30, 38, 55.

59. *Harris survey on quality of life: Ibid.*, p. 111.

60. *Harris survey on comparisons with young: Ibid.*, p. 45.

60. *forced home ownership:* Bernard Benjamin Hoffman, Jr., *Forced Home Ownership* (Syracuse, N.Y.: Syracuse University, 1967).

62. *Rainwater finding:* cited in James T. Mathieu, "Housing Preferences and Satisfactions," in M. Powell Lawton et al., *Community Planning for an Aging Society: Designing Services and Facilities* (Stroudsburg, Pa.; Dowden, Hutchinson & Ross, 1976), p. 160.

62. *Mathieu on Safety: Ibid.*, p. 170.

62. *elderly criminal victimization sources: In Search of Security: A National Perspective on Elderly Crime Victimization*, Report of the Select Committee on Aging, Ninety-fifty Congress, First Session, April 1977, Comm. Pub. No. 95–87; Jack Goldsmith and Sharon S. Goldsmith, *Crime and the Elderly* (Lexington, Mass.: Heath, 1976); and Marlene A. Young Rifai, *Justice and Older Americans* (Lexington, Mass.: Heath, 1977).

62. *elderly victimization rates: In Search of Security*, pp. 5, 8, 19.

63. *chapter on fear of crime: Ibid.*, pp. 28–46.

64. *Mayer quote:* Martin Mayer, *The Builders: Houses, People, Neighborhoods, Governments, Money* (New York: Norton, 1978), p. 419.

Chapter 4. A Self-Portrait of Housing
(pp. 69–84)

69. *Butler quote:* Robert N. Butler, *Why Survive? Growing Old in America* (New York: Harper & Row, 1975), p. 107.

70. *Butler quotes: Ibid.*, pp. 108, 109.
70. *social work perspective:* For a lucid exposition of this theme see C. L.Estes, "Goal Displacement in Community Planning for the Elderly," in M. Powell Lawton et al., *Community Planning For an Aging Society: Designing Services and Facilities* (Stroudsburg, Pa., Dowden, Hutchinson & Ross, 1976), p. 313.
71. *elderly don't need social services:* Richard S. Sterne et al., *The Urban Elderly Poor* (Lexington, Mass.: Heath, 1974), pp. 25–28.
73. *property tax relief programs:* Abt Associates, Inc., *Property Tax Relief Programs for the Elderly*, Final Report, U.S. Department of Housing and Urban Development, Office of Policy Development and Research, November 1975.
81. *Butler quote:* Robert N. Butler, *Why Survive?*, p. 109.

Chapter 5. The Experts' View (pp. 85–123)

85. *Glazer citation:* Nathan Glazer, "Housing Policy and the Family," in *Journal of Marriage and the Family*, February 1967.
86. *definition of housing:* an excellent treatment of this subject is found in T.L.C. Duncan, *Measuring Housing Quality: A Study of Methods* (Birmingham, England: Center for Urban and Regional Studies, University of Birmingham, 1971), pp. xi–xii.
87. *Smith citation:* Wallace F. Smith, *Housing: the Social and Economic Elements* (Berkeley: University of California Press, 1970), pp. 3–10.
87. *Grisby and Rosenburg citation:* William G. Grigsby and Louis Rosenburg, *Urban Housing Policy*, Center for Urban Policy Research, Rutgers University (New York: APS Publications, 1975), pp. 31–57.
88. *1844 survey:* Robert H. Bremner, *From the Depths: The Discovery of Poverty in the United States* (New York: New York University Press, 1956), p. 37.
88. *history of housing standards:* The history of housing standards is discussed in the following sources: T.L.C. Duncan, *op. cit., passim;* William C. Baer, "The Evolution of Housing

Indicators and Housing Standards: Some Lessons for the Future," in *Public Policy*, Summer 1976, pp. 361–93; and *Annual Housing Survey: 1973, Part B. Indicators of Housing and Neighborhood Quality*. U.S. Department of Commerce, Bureau of the Census, Series H–150–73B, 1975, p. xiv.

89. *statistics on condition unreliable: Measuring the Quality of Housing: An Appraisal of Census Statistics and Methods,* U.S. Bureau of the Census Working Paper No. 25, Washington, D.C., 1967.

90. *A.P.H.A. appraisal method:* T.L.C. Duncan, *op. cit.,* pp. 25–34; see also *An Appraisal Method for Measuring the Quality of Housing: A Yardstick for Health Officers, Housing Officials and Planners* (New York: American Public Health Association, 1945); and *Housing: Basic Health Principles & Recommended Ordinance.* (Washington, D.C.: American Public Health Association, 1971).

90. *codes:* Harold L. Wolman, *Housing and Housing Policy in the U.S. and the U.K.* (Lexington, Mass.: Heath, 1975), p. 87. Despite the variability in the definition and enforcement of code standards, we asked our respondents if they had recently been cited for one or more code violations to discover how extensive this might be. Overall, about one in seven elderly people have undergone a recent housing inspection; of those who had been inspected, one-fourth were compelled to correct a code violation. In absolute numbers, 67 elderly homeowners of our sample of 1,575 were required to make repairs in light of an inspection. Twenty-three of them live in Dayton, in which housing authorities had just completed an intensive citywide code enforcement program. Against this particular standard, even after a very intensive code enforcement program in Dayton, only 10 percent of the elderly homeowners were found guilty of a code violation. In other sites, the figures were lower.

91. *Kain and Quigley citation:* John F. Kain and John M. Quigley, "Measuring the Value of Housing Quality," in John F. Kain (ed.), *Essays on Urban Spatial Structure* (Cambridge, Mass., Ballinger, 1975), pp. 261–76.

91. *New Haven study:* D. M. Grether and Peter Miezkowski,

"Determinants of Real Estate Values," in *Journal of Urban Economics*, January 1974, pp. 127–45.

91. *Boston study*: Ann B. Schnare and Raymond J. Struyk, "Segmentation in Urban Housing Markets," in *Journal of Urban Economics*, April 1976, pp. 146–66.

92. *1970 estimate*: No direct measure of physical condition was reported in the 1970 Census of Housing, but indirect estimates were made. See *Plumbing Facilities and Estimates of Dilapidated Housing*, U.S. Bureau of the Census, Vol. 6, 1973.

92. *Baer quote*: William C. Baer, *op. cit.*, p. 375.

92. *Weicher citation*: John C. Weicher, "A Decent Home for Every American," in *Federal Home Loan Bank Board Journal*, August 1977, pp. 7–10. See also John C. Weicher, "'A Decent Home': An Assessment of Progress Toward the National Housing Goal and Policies Adopted to Achieve It," in Donald Phares (ed.), *A Decent Home and Environment: Housing Urban America* (Cambridge, Mass.: Ballinger, 1977), pp. 138–55.

94. *Struyk citation*: Raymond J. Struyk, *The Housing Situation of Elderly Americans* (Washington, D.C.: The Urban Institute, 1976).

95. *history of overcrowding*: William C. Baer, *op. cit.*, pp. 375–81.

96. *Pruitt-Igoe overcrowding*: Eugene J. Meehan, *Public Housing Policy: Convention Versus Reality* (New Brunswick, N.J.: Center for Urban Policy Research, 1975), p. 37.

96. *Hong Kong housing density*: D. W. Drakakis-Smith, *Housing Provision in Metropolitan Hong Kong* (Hong Kong: Center of Asian Studies, University of Hong Kong, 1973), pp. 35, 40, 78.

97. *"ability to pay" criterion*: William C. Baer, *op. cit.*, pp. 381–85.

98. *neighborhood quality*: T.L.C. Duncan, *op. cit.*, pp. 82–102.

99. *Muth citation*: Richard F. Muth, *Cities and Housing* (Chicago: University of Chicago Press, 1969), pp. 115–30.

99. *Hughes and Bleakly citation*: James W. Hughes and Kenneth D. Bleakly, Jr., *Urban Homesteading* (New Brunswick, N.J.:

Center for Urban Policy Research, Rutgers University, 1975), pp. 46–54.

112. *Muth quote:* Richard F. Muth, *Cities and Housing: The Spatial Pattern of Urban Residential Land Use* (Chicago: University of Chicago Press, 1969), p. 115.

112. *income and housing condition: Ibid.,* Chapter 6 and Charles L. Leven et al., *Neighborhood Change: Lessons in the Dynamics of Urban Decay* (New York: Praeger, 1976).

114. *housing quality and housing price:* John F. Kain and John M. Quigley, "Measuring the Value of Housing Quality," in John F. Kain (ed.), *Essays in Urban Spatial Structure* (Cambridge, Mass.: Ballinger, 1975), pp. 261–76.

118. *age of housing and housing quality:* cited in Richard F. Muth, *op. cit.,* Chapters 6 and 10.

119. *neighborhood income and housing quality:* Richard F. Muth, *loc. cit.* and Charles L. Leven et al., *op. cit.*

119. *race and housing quality:* Charles L. Leven et al., *op. cit.*

121. *blacks pay more for housing:* Richard F. Muth, *op. cit., passim.,* and John F. Kain and John M. Quigley, *Housing Markets and Racial Discrimination* (New York: National Bureau of Economic Research, 1975).

Chapter 6. Lay versus Expert (pp. 124–32)

130. *Rochester elderly:* Richard S. Sterne et al., *The Urban Elderly Poor: Racial and Bureaucratic Conflict* (Lexington, Mass.: Heath, 1974).

130. *Los Angeles County elderly:* Mark J. Riesenfeld et al., "Perceptions of Public Service Needs: The Urban Elderly and the Public Agency," in *Gerontologist,* Summer 1972, Part I, pp. 185–90.

131. *public housing quote:* Alvin Rabushka and William G. Weissert, *Caseworkers or Police? How Tenants See Public Housing* (Stanford, Calif.: Hoover Institution Press, 1977), p. xvii.

Chapter 7. What's in the Way? (pp. 135–52)

135. *Binstock and Levin quote:* Robert H. Binstock and Martin A. Levin, "The Political Dilemmas of Intervention Policies," in

Robert H. Binstock and Ethel Shanas (eds.), *Handbook of Aging and the Social Sciences* (New York: Van Nostrand Reinhold, 1976), p. 511.

137. *property tax relief: Property Tax Relief Programs for the Elderly,* prepared for U.S. Department of Housing and Urban Development by Abt Associates, Inc. (Washington, D.C.: U.S. Government Printing Office, November 1975).

138. *Aaron quote:* Henry J. Aaron, *Shelter and Subsidies: Who Benefits from Federal Housing Policies?* (Washington, D.C.: The Brookings Institution, 1972), p. 11.

142. *failure of housing programs:* A substantial literature documents the failures of federal housing and community development programs. Several excellent examples of this literature include Martin Anderson, *The Federal Bulldozer* (New York: McGraw-Hill, 1967); *Housing in the Seventies: A Report of the National Housing Policy Review* (Washington, D.C.: U.S. Department of Housing and Urban Development, 1974) and Lawrence M. Friedman, *Government and Slum Housing: A Century of Frustration* (Chicago: Rand McNally, 1968).

142. *Farmers Home Administration grants and loans:* See *The Budget of the United States Government, Fiscal Year 1980, Appendix,* pp. 161-62, 164-65.

142. *rural housing improvements:* James E. Montgomery, "Housing of the Rural Aged," in E. Grant Youmans (ed.), *Older Rural Americans: A Sociological Perspective* (Lexington: University of Kentucky Press, 1967), p. 178.

147. *EHAP results: Experimental Housing Allowance Program: A 1979 Report of Findings,* U.S. Department of Housing and Urban Development, April 1979, p. 28.

Chapter 8. What's To Be Done? (pp. 153-68)

155. *problem of implementation:* Implementation of public programs is being increasingly recognized as an important subfield in public policy analysis. Several useful books and essays include Jeffrey L. Pressman and Aaron Wildavsky, *Implementation* (Berkeley: University of California Press, 1973); Eugene Bardach, *The Implementation Game* (Cam-

bridge, Mass.: M.I.T. Press, 1977); and the entire issue of *Public Policy*, Spring 1978.

155. *opposition to Social Security costs:* Martha Derthick, "How Easy Votes on Social Security Came to an End," *The Public Interest*, Number 54, Winter 1979.

157. *reverse annuities:* Memorandum SA No. 523, Federal Home Loan Bank Board, December 15, 1978, "Alternative Mortgage Instruments," See also "Reverse Mortgages: Income for Paid-up Homeowners," in *Changing Times*, August 1978, pp. 17–18.

157. French policy: *France: News in Brief*, publication of the Press and Information Division of the French Embassy, New York, August–September 1978, p. 6.

160. *housing inspection programs:* Mathematica Policy Research, Inc., *A Study of Home Inspection and Warranty Programs*, Vol. I., submitted to the U.S. Department of Housing and Urban Development, June 1977.

162. *mandatory retirement:* Examples of these contentions are found in Erdman Palmore, "Compulsory Versus Flexible Retirement: Issues and Facts," in Bill D. Bell (ed.), *Social Gerontology: Significant Developments in the Field of Aging* (Springfield, Ill.: Charles C. Thomas, 1976), pp. 172–77; Robert M. Macdonald, *Mandatory Retirement and the Law* (Washington, D.C.: American Enterprise Institute, 1978); and Barry R. Chiswick and Carmel U. Chiswick, "On Benefits of Mandatory Retirement," *New York Times*, November 12, 1977, p. 21.

163. *minimum wage laws:* Walter E. Williams, *Youth and Minority Employment* (Stanford: Hoover Institution Press, 1977); Edward M. Gramlich, "Testimony Before the Subcommittee on Labor Standards of the House, Education, and Labor Committee, March 9, 1977," in Hearings on H.R. 3744, *Fair Labor Standards Amendments of 1977*, 95th Congress, 1st session, pp. 232–236; Thomas G. Moore, "The Effect of Minimum Wages on Teenage Unemployment Rates," *Journal of Political Economy* (July/August 1971), pp. 897–902; and Jacob Mincer, "Unemployment Effects of Minimum Wages," *Journal of Political Economy* (August 1976), pp. 87–105.

164. *data on elderly tax exemption:* Federal Council on Aging,

The Impact of the Tax Structure on the Elderly (Washington, D.C.: U.S. Government Printing Office, 1975), p. 49.

166. *neighborhood transition:* Charles L. Leven et al., *Neighborhood Change: Lessons in the Dynamics of Urban Decay* (New York: Praeger, 1976).

Appendix C
A Statistical Explanation of Housing Condition
(pp. 176–80)

177. *owner's estimate of worth of home:* John F. Kain and John M. Quigley, "Note on Owner's Estimate of House Value," in *Journal of American Statistical Association,* 1972, pp. 803–6.

178. *two-stage least squares analysis:* Eric A. Hanushek and John E. Jackson, *Statistical Methods for Social Scientists* (New York: Academic Press, 1977), Chapters 8 and 9.

179. *hypothesis testing:* Potluri Rao and Roger LeRoy Miller, *Applied Econometrics* (Belmont, Calif.: Wadsworth, 1971), Chapter 6.

Select List of References on Aging

BAUMHOVER, LORIN A. and JOAN DECHOW JONES, eds. *Handbook of American Aging Programs.* Westport, Conn.: Greenwood, 1977.

BELL, BILL D., ed. *Contemporary Social Gerontology: Significant Developments in the Field of Aging.* Springfield, Ill.: Charles C Thomas, 1976.

BINSTOCK, ROBERT H. and ETHEL SHANAS, eds. *Handbook of Aging and the Social Sciences.* New York: Van Nostrand Reinhold, 1976.

BIRREN, JAMES and K. W. SCHAIE, eds. *Handbook of Aging and the Individual.* New York: Van Nostrand Reinhold, 1976.

BUTLER, ROBERT N. *Why Survive? Being Old in America.* New York: Harper & Row, 1975.

CALA, MICHAEL with SUSAN LOB and MARINA SROGE. *The Older Person's Handbook.* New York: A Mutual Aid Project Handbook, Citizens Committee for New York City, 1978.

DAVIS, RICHARD H. *Aging: Prospects and Issues.* Los Angeles: Ethel Percy Andrus Gerontology Center, University of Southern California, 1973.

HARRIS, CHARLES S. *Fact Book on Aging: A Profile of America's Older Population.* Washington, D.C.: National Council on the Aging, February 1978.

HENDRICKS, JON and C. DAVIS HENDRICKS. *Aging in Mass Society: Myths and Realities.* Cambridge, Mass.: Winthrop, 1977.

NORBACK, CRAIG T. AND PETER NORBACK. *The Older Americans Handbook.* New York: Van Nostrand Reinhold, 1977.

PALMORE, ERDMAN, ed. *Normal Aging: Reports from the Duke Longitudinal Study, 1955–1969.* Durham, N.C.: Duke University Press, 1970.

RILEY, MATILDA W. et al., eds. *Aging and Society. Volume I. An Inventory of Research Findings.* New York: Russell Sage, 1968.

RILEY, MATILDA W., JOHN W. RILEY, JR., and MARILYN E. JOHNSON. *Aging and Society. Volume II. Aging and the Professions.* New York: Russell Sage, 1969.

RILEY, MATILDA W., MARILYN E. JOHNSON, and ANNE FONER. *Aging and Society. Volume III. A Sociology of Age Stratification.* New York: Russell Sage, 1972.

Sourcebook on Aging. Chicago: Marquis Academic Media, 1977.

TIBBITS, CLARK, ed. *Handbook of Social Gerontology: Societal Aspects of Aging.* Chicago: University of Chicago Press, 1960.

WOODRUFF, DIANA and JAMES BIRREN, eds. *Aging: Scientific Perspectives and Social Issues.* New York: Van Nostrand Reinhold, 1975.

Index

Aaron, Henry J., 138
Administration on Aging, 5
  creation of, 28
  growth in expenditures of, 29
  programs of, 28–31
Age Discrimination in Employment Act, 29
Aged: see Elderly
Aging, government involvement in, 24, 27–31; see also Gerontology
American Aging Association, 23
American Association of Retired Persons, 23
American Geriatrics Society, 23
American Public Health Association (APHA), 89–91
  Appraisal Method, 90
  overcrowding limit, 96
Ancient society, life span in, 21–22
Annual Housing Survey, 6, 11, 89, 94–95, 98
Atchley, Robert, 47
Attitudes toward the elderly, 58–60; see also Stereotypes

Bacon, Roger, 27
Baer, William C., 92
Black elderly Americans, 36–37
  housing condition of, 116–17
  special needs of, 57
The Black Elderly: A Guide for Practitioners, 57
Bleakly, Kenneth D., Jr., 99
Building codes, 31
Butler, Robert N., 8, 47, 69–70, 81

Califano, Joseph A., Jr., 3
Capital-gains tax on sale of elderly-owned residence, 159–60
Carter, Jimmy, 29
Community Development Block Grant, 141
Comprehensive Employment and Training Act (CETA) 1978, 29
Condition of housing, 88–95
  and affordability, 86
  improvement in, 11, 92–94, 97–98
  objective statement of, 102–104: basic facilities, 102; health or safety hazards, 103; long-term repair needs, 103
  standards of, 87–95: historical changes in, 88–92; monetary approach to, 88, 91–92; social-hygiene approach to, 88–91
  statistical explanation of, 176–80
Congressional Budget Office study (1977), 7, 50

Consumer Price Index (CPI)
  housing component, 7
  rise in since 1950, 7
Contracting firms, elderly homeowners and, 82–84
Crime, fear of, 11, 62–63, 156, 161
Critical defects
  concept of, 111
  factors associated with, 112–23
  presence of, 126, 156

Dancy, Joseph, Jr., 57
Dayton
  code enforcement in, 140
  homeowner opinions of government programs in, 148–50
  population, 39
  sampling procedure in, 40–41
Decay, of housing stock, 137
Dilapidation, as a housing deficiency, 86, 89, 96
  decline in, 92–93
Discrimination against the elderly, 74, 162
Double personal exemption, 9, 164
  replacement with tax credit, 164–65

Elderly
  characteristics of, 35–37
  employment of, 8, 12, 24, 74: decline in self-, 12; historical decline in, 24, 26
  geographical distribution of, 36
  geographical mobility of, 7, 9
  health of, 6, 10, 36
  home equity of, 158
  income of, 5–6, 9–10, 48–49
  isolation of, 7–8, 12
  life expectancy of, 21–22, 37
  living arrangements of, 4–5, 26
  marital status of, 36
  media coverage of, 3–4
  minorities, 36–37, 57
  negative images of, 4, 5–9, 13–14, 33, 58–59, 72, 153
  numbers of, 20–22, 24
  political power of, 24
  poverty of, 5–6, 9
  racial composition of, 36
  relations with children, 12
  residential patterns of, 4–5, 36–37
  retirement practices of, 25–26
  in rural areas, 32, 37
  sex composition of, 35–36
  standard view of, 5–9

Elderly (cont.)
    tax benefits of, 9, 11, 50
    women, 35–36
Elderly homeowners; see also Homes, elderly-
    owned
    age distribution of, 43
    black, 58
    description of, 14, 33
    geographical mobility of, 72
    government programs for, 32, 156–65
    problems of, 70
Elderly homeowners, in seven sites
    assets of, 51
    contact with children, 46–47
    educational background of, 55–56
    fear of crime among, 63, 72
    geographical mobility of, 72
    happiness with neighborhood among, 62–63
    health of, 54
    home equity of, 52, 159
    income of, 51
    income potential of, 52–53
    isolation of, 46–57
    living arrangements of, 44–45
    maintenance and repair expenditures of,
        81–82
    marital status of, 44–45
    physical mobility of, 35
    positive image of aging among, 59–60
    poverty among, 53
    program knowledge of, 146
    program participation of, 146
    program preferences of, 148–49
    racial attitudes of, 62, 64
    satisfaction with home of, 61, 72
    self-reliant values of, 47, 59, 147–54
    social relations of, 46–47
    tenure of residence of, 72
    use of contractors by, 82–84
    wealth of, 51
Experimental Housing Allowance Program
    (EHAP), 101, 147, 173
Externalities in the housing market, 138–40,
    155

Facts and Figures on Older Americans, 5
Family structure, change in, 26–27
Farmers Home Administration (FHA), 32
    FHA Home Repair Loan Program (Section
        504), 141–42, 147
Federal Council on Aging, 28
Federal government
    expenditures on elderly, 3, 30–31
    expenditures on Social Security, 20, 29
Federal Home Loan Bank Board, 157
Fischer, David Hackett, 25
Florida, aged population in, 19, 37
Ford, Gerald, 19
Forced homeownership, thesis of, 11–12,
    60–61

Foster Grandparents program, 29

Gerontological Society, 23
Gerontology, 22–24
Glazer, Nathan, 85
Golden, Herbert, 57
Goldwater, Barry, 20
Government intervention
    competing objectives of, 135, 155
    and compulsion, 140, 145
    implementation problems of, 135, 141,
        144–48, 155
    rationale for, 137–40
    successful principles of, 155
Gray Panthers, 23
Grigsby William, 87

Harris (Louis) Survey on Aging, 11, 12, 34–
    35, 46, 50–51, 55, 59, 63
Health, subjective assessment of, 54
    and housing condition, 114–115
Home, decent
    definition of, 85, 92, 124, 155
    goal of, 138
    meeting goal of, 92, 124
    standards of, 85–86
Home inspections, 160–61
Homes, elderly-owned
    age of, 6, 10, 72
    in central cities, 137–38, 166–67
    condition of, 94
    conservation of, 136
    equity in, 10, 11
    number of, 5, 136
    repair and maintenance of, 11, 34, 136
    rising costs of living in, 7
    in rural areas, 7, 32, 142
    satisfaction with, 12
    value of, 5–7
Homes, elderly-owned, in seven sites
    comparison of owner and expert ratings,
        126–29
    condition of, 75–80, 104–10, 124, 176–80:
        and age of head, 117–20; and age of
        house, 114, 120; and community income,
        119; and education, 115–16, 120; and
        health, 80, 114–14, 120; and home equity,
        114, 122; and income, 80, 112–13, 122;
        owners' assessment of, 75–80, 84; and
        poverty, 123; and race, 116–17, 121–22;
        and racial composition of neighborhood,
        119; and wealth, 112–14, 122
    contractor work on, 82
    experts' ratings of, 100–10, 124
    maintenance and repair expenditures on,
        81–82
    overcrowding in, 74, 97
    size of, 74
Housing
    and ability to pay, 97–98

basic facilities in, 86
codes, 31, 32, 90, 138, 140, 144–45, 160
condition: *see* Condition of housing
conservation, 137
definition of, 86–97
and government, 31–32, 136–52
and neighborhood quality, 98–99
overcrowding in, 95–97
rising costs of, 137
standards, 87–100, 166
Housing Act of 1949, 85, 138
Housing Act of 1954, 32, 90
Housing and Community Development Act of 1974, 98
Housing Evaluation Form (HEF), 111, 128, 173–75
derivation of, 101
elements contained in, 101
reliability of, 101
results from, 105–10
Housing Improvement Program (Boston), 141
Hughes, James W., 99

Income, impact on neighborhood, 112
"Independence ethic," 147–48
In-kind income, 9, 48, 119
Isolation, 7–8, 12, 46–47

Jackson, Jacquelyne Johnson, 57
Journal of Gerontology, 23

Kain, John F., 91

Levin, Martin A., 135
Life expectancy, 21–22

Maintenance and repair expenditures in seven sites, 81–82
Mathieu, James T., 62
Mayer, Martin, 11, 64
Medicaid, 9, 29, 30
Medicare, 9, 29, 30
Meehan, Eugene J., 96
Minimum wages, 163–64
proposed abolition of, 164
Mismatch: *see* Needs/preferences mismatch
Moon, Marilyn, 49, 52
Muth, Richard F., 99, 112
The Myth and Reality of Aging in America, 35

National Association of Retired Federal Employees, 23
National Caucus on the Black Aged, 23, 57
National Center for Health Statistics, 6
National Center on Black Aged, 23
National Council on Senior Citizens, 23
National Council on the Aging, 23, 31, 34
National Institute on Aging, 8, 29, 69
National Institutes of Health, 29
National Journal, 4

National Retired Teachers Association, 23
Needs, 15, 16–18, 128
concept of, 16, 125
objective nature of, 16, 18, 126
Needs/preferences mismatch, 16, 129–32, 152, 156, 167
for housing condition, 125–31
Neighborhood
and changing populations, 100, 119
crime, 11, 62–64
decline, 99–100
and declining community income, 119
and deferral of maintenance, 99
racial tension in, 11, 62, 64–65
satisfaction with, 11
Neighborhood quality, as a housing deficiency, 98–100
New Republic, 4
New Ulm (Minnesota)
description of, 4
homeowner opinions of government programs in, 156
population, 39
sampling procedure in, 42
New York Association for Improving the Condition of the Poor, 88
Newsweek, 3

Old age assistance, history of, 27–28
Older Americans Act (1965), 28–30, 142
Orangeburg County (South Carolina)
description of 43, 121
home condition in, 77–78, 106, 111, 122, 128
population, 39
poverty in, 53
sampling procedure in, 42–43
Orshansky, Mollie, 49
Overcrowding, as a housing deficiency, 86, 95–97

Philadelphia
description of, 40, 72
home condition in, 106
homeowner opinions of government programs in, 150
population, 39
sampling procedure in, 40
Pittsfield
description of, 41–42, 72
home condition in, 106
homeowner opinions of government programs in, 148
population, 39
Plumbing facilities as a housing deficiency, 86, 89, 92–93
Policy, public
and elderly-owned housing, 136, 140–42, 148–49, 156–65
and housing, 137–38, 140–44

Policy, public (*cont.*)
  and individual preferences, 136, 155
  successful principles of, 155
Poverty
  and the elderly, 5–6, 47–50
  and elderly-owned housing, 123, 166
  and the Great Depression, 26
  and retirement, 21
Pratt, Henry J., 19
Preferences, 15–17, 128
  definition of, 15–16, 125–26
  subjective nature of, 15, 17–18, 125
Programs, government
  housing, 140–44
  participation in, 146
  preferences for, 148–49
Property tax relief, 11, 73, 137, 143–44
  circuit-breakers, 73, 143, 143*n*
  deferral of taxes, 73, 144, 158–59
  freezing of taxes, 144
  homestead exemptions, 73, 143, 143*n*
  knowledge of, 146
Property Tax Relief Programs for the Elderly, 143
Public housing
  for the elderly, 29
  in Hong Kong, 85, 96–97

Quality of housing: *see* Condition of housing
Quigley, John M., 91

Race issue, 56–57, 116–17, 119, 121–22
Rainwater, Lee, 62
Reagan, Ronald, 19
Real Property Inventories (RPI) program, 88, 95
Rehabilitation grants (Section 115), 141
Rehabilitation loans (Section 312), 141
Rent/income ratio as a measure of housing inadequacy, 86, 97–98
Retired Senior Volunteer Program (RSVP), 29
Retirement
  among New England clergy, 25
  attitudes toward historically, 24–25
  early, 43
  growth of in modern America, 26
  mandatory, 8, 12, 25, 161–63
  and poverty, 26, 47
Revenue Act of 1978, 159
Reverse annuities, 157–58
Roosevelt, Franklin D., 23, 24
Rosenburg, Louis, 87

Sample design, 40–43, 171–72
San Francisco
  age of homes, 72
  description of, 41
  home values in, 159
  homeowner opinions of government programs in, 151

sampling procedure in, 41
Schulz, James H., 48
Site selection, criteria for, 39
Smith, Wallace, 87
The Social Forces in Later Life, 47
Social Security
  benefits from, 12, 43: growth in, 20, 146; indexing, 9, 11, 73
  European counterparts, 23, 27–28
  financial viability of, 19, 21, 153
  outlays, size of, 20, 29–30, 155
  political support for, 19–20
  tax receipts, 20
Social Security Act, 19, 23, 28
Social Security Administration, *1968 Survey of the Aged*, 48
Social work perspective, 70–71
Standard Metropolitan Statistical Area (SMSA), 39–40, 171
Stereotypes of aging, negative, 4, 5–9, 58–59
Struyk, Raymond, 94
Supplemental Security Income (SSI) program, 29–30, 49
Survey research, underreporting of income in, 48

Time, 3
Tulsa
  age of homes in, 72
  description of, 41
  homeowner opinions of government programs in, 151
  population, 39

United States Congress, 85
U.S. Bureau of the Census, 48
  Census of Housing (1940), 44–49
  Census of Housing (1950), 89
  Census of Housing (1960), 89
  Census of Housing (1970), 6, 89
  Survey of family income, 49
U.S. Department of Health, Education and Welfare, 3
U.S. Department of Housing and Urban Development, 35, 60, 89, 140, 143, 160
U.S. House of Representatives, Select Committee on Aging, 24
U.S. Public Health Service, 90
U.S. Senate Labor Committee, Special Staff on Aging, 29
U.S. Senate, Special Committee on Aging, 5, 24
The Urban Elderly Poor, 56

Weicher, John C., 92, 94
Welfare, and liens on property, 72–74
White House Conference on Aging (1961), 28
Why Survive? Being Old in America, 47, 69

Zoning, 31, 138